ALSO BY CAL RIPKEN, JR.

The Only Way I Know

PLAY BASEBALL

THE RIPKEN WAY

PLAY BASEBALL

Cal Ripken, Jr., and Bill Ripken

with Larry Burke

THE RIPKEN WAY

263

The Complete Illustrated Guide
to the Fundamentals

BALLANTINE BOOKS   NEW YORK

A Ballantine Book
Published by The Random House Publishing Group
Copyright © 2004 by Ripken Baseball, Inc.

Published in the United States by Ballantine Books, an imprint of The Random House
Publishing Group, a division of Random House, Inc., New York, and simultaneously
in Canada by Random House of Canada Limited, Toronto.

Ballantine and colophon are registered trademarks of Random House, Inc.

www.ballantinebooks.com

A Library of Congress Control Number can be obtained from the publisher upon request.

ISBN 978-0-8129-7050-0

This work was originally published in hardcover by Random House, an imprint of
The Random House Publishing Group, a division of Random House, Inc., in 2004.

Manufactured in the United States of America

First Trade Paperback Edition: February 2005

9 8 7 6 5

Book design by BTDNYC

ACKNOWLEDGMENTS

So many people have contributed to the creation of this book, and we want to thank all of them for their invaluable assistance: John Habyan, Mark Parent, Joe Orsulak, our new team at Ripken Baseball, Bill Wood, Larry Burke, Scott Waxman, Zach Schisgal, and everyone at Random House who made this project a success.

The photographs are by Bill Wood.

CONTENTS

PLAY BASEBALL
THE **RIPKEN** WAY

THE RIPKEN WAY

Our Teaching Philosophy

By Cal Ripken, Jr.

There has always been something special about the game of baseball. That something is hard to define, or maybe the things that make it so special are so broad and deep that what appeals to one person is completely different from what appeals to another.

The game is complicated by the nature of its skills, rules, and seemingly endless strategies. We as people help to complicate things. We're always trying to figure out how to do things better. Baseball, by its sheer nature, demands to be figured out. That's the part that appeals to us.

We've spent our entire lives trying to figure out the game of baseball, and it continues to teach us the same way it taught our father, Cal Ripken, Sr. We have a couple of generations of knowledge and experience, from the earliest levels to the most advanced. Our whole family has a passion for the game and a deep understanding of it. We know of the simple joys and the simple fundamentals as well as the most complicated strategies and the most sophisticated instruction. We can't say we know everything about the game (no one can make that claim), but we know a lot, and we have a great love of the game.

Before I get into the Ripken Way, because my job here is to introduce that, let me say one thing: The whole idea of having a Ripken Way bothers me a little. To me baseball is a great game that has certain rules, and the nature of the game allows us all to play it. There are no size restrictions or age limitations, and best of all there's not one way in which you must go about playing this game. Dad used to always say that there's more than one way to skin a cat. Well, maybe this isn't the most modern of sayings, but it's the meaning that counts. It was a philosophy that Dad believed in, and he basically lived his life that way.

So you can see that when we talk about the Ripken Way there's a potential conflict. On one side we're saying that there's more than one way to do things, and on the other side we're implying that there's this one way to teach and play baseball. But here's why there is not a conflict: Part of the Ripken Way is to recognize and understand that there's more than one way of doing things. We celebrate the differences in people; we think that makes the game better. We encourage you to tap into your own set of talents, because the goal is to make individual contributions for the good of the team. By tapping into your specific skill set, not only will you make contributions to the team, you might even make a bigger contribution to the game itself. You might change the way it's played or the way it's viewed. You might make it better for everyone.

If I were to explain in one sentence what the Ripken Way means, it would be this: Be yourself, be open to the experience and wisdom of others who have played the game, apply the proven fundamentals of the game, keep things simple, and remember that baseball is a game and it's supposed to be fun. Okay, it was very hard to put that into one sentence without making it a compound sentence, and I still left out a big part of the Ripken Way. We think it's very important to explain the *why*. I was a Why Kid growing up. I always drove everyone crazy by asking them "Why?" but I discovered that real learning takes place when someone explains the spirit of a decision or a lesson. Dad explained everything. He had the patience to explain because he knew the value of the explanation. We value that as well, and at our camps and clinics we encourage the kids to ask us and our instructors "Why?" If we're teaching things a certain way, we should know why.

To give you a little context about the Ripken Way: Our Dad, Cal Sr., was a major part of the Baltimore Orioles organization for thirty-seven years, as a player, manager, coach, and scout. During that period the Orioles were considered a model organization. Because of their success over a long period of time, the Oriole Way developed. It was a formula for playing solid, fundamental baseball, but at its core it was nothing more than a lot of good baseball people doing their jobs on a daily basis. Through trial and error, and by keeping what worked and discarding what didn't, the Orioles developed a system. The key to this system was the people. There was tremendous stability in the personnel. I remember Dad saying that for a period of seven years virtually everyone served in their same role. Dad was one of those people.

But over time, as things changed, what was once known as the Oriole Way became diluted. Dad passed on many of the principles of the Oriole Way to Bill and me and to a great many members of our instructing staff. Over the years, as Dad added his own views and philosophy from his vast experience in the game, it became known as the Ripken Way. Bill's and my success added to the meaning of the Ripken Way—among the two of us and Dad we have eighty-eight years of experience in professional baseball, fifty of them in the big leagues—but it really came from a bunch of good baseball people, especially Dad, passing on what worked and what didn't. We'll take the credit on Dad's behalf, and through the Ripken Way we'll continue to pass on that wisdom of baseball.

The Ripken Way consists of four basic points:

KEEP IT SIMPLE

Basic lessons are critical for allowing a young person to develop a foundation on which to build. Teachings or drills that are too technical and challenging can frustrate and confuse a young player.

Fundamentals are the building blocks for playing the game of baseball at any level. If a young player has not been introduced to the fundamental skills—and has not had the opportunity to practice those skills over and over—when it comes time to introduce more advanced concepts, such as turning the double play, the player is inevitably going to struggle and become frustrated. Bill often tells our campers that he can watch teams warm up before a game and pick out which team is going to win just by watching them play catch. The team that plays catch the best will win. While that may be an oversimplification, it's not far from the truth.

The word "play," as in *play* catch, is important. You don't go out and *do* baseball. You *play* baseball. Dad used to emphasize the playing aspect. It's very simple: To *play* baseball, you need to throw, catch, hit, and run. The more you play, the better you get. Playing, by definition, is meant to be fun. Young people by nature are eager to learn and improve. With proper guidance and an emphasis on fundamentals, they will continue to improve as they *play*. The improvement results in a natural progression in which young players can complete more difficult and complicated tasks on the field. That success quenches their innate desire to learn and improve and keeps them coming back for more.

However, it's not enough just to *play*. Without a foundation on which to build—fundamental lessons—simply playing can lead to frustration. To be successful on the baseball field, you don't have to do anything extraordinary, though. Dad always talked about making the game look easy. If you catch a ground ball and make a strong, accurate throw to retire the batter, you're doing your job. Because you made the "routine" play look routine, your efforts might go unnoticed. But Dad would say that you did it the right way.

Dad loved to analyze the game of baseball. He was a great thinker. Fortunately, he passed that ability on to both Bill and me. There are times when you can overanalyze and get bogged down in analysis. Dad did not analyze the game to make it more complicated, though. It was his mind-set to break the game down to its fundamental bases. His style of teaching was to reduce a complicated topic to something simple and then articulate it point by point. If you can break the game down to its simplest skills, baseball becomes easier to understand—for the eight-year-old, the eighteen-year-old, or the twenty-eight-year-old.

EXPLAIN THE WHY

Anyone can tell you how to do something, but only true teachers can tell you why it's important to complete a task in a certain way. If you can communicate a concept to a young baseball player and "explain the why" behind the concept, it gives you credibility as a teacher. In general, kids have an innate desire to understand "the why." When a parent, coach, or teacher can communicate that message effectively, the child becomes satisfied and is much more happy to perform as instructed.

Every day, possibly every minute, a parent somewhere is telling a child, "Do this" or "Do that." And nine times out of ten the kid responds by asking, "Why?" Believe it or not, this scenario was played out occasionally in the Ripken household. Mom certainly heard that question frequently, and human nature dictated that sometimes she would get frustrated and reply, "Because I said so!" Does that sound familiar? I would be willing to bet that every parent has uttered a similar response at least once. It certainly is a concise, effective way to get a point across without having to take the time to explain it.

As parents, we are the ultimate teachers, because we're responsible for educating our kids about virtually every subject imaginable almost all the time. Being a parent—a friend, teacher, and role model all wrapped into one—is possibly the most demanding job there is. Therefore, it's perfectly understandable when an occasional "Because I said so" comes out of our mouths. Why do you think that happens only occasionally? It's because as parents we understand that learning can't take place when a child simply follows directions. Learning occurs when there's an understanding.

Let's look at baseball as an example. Watching a major league player make a play on television might be a helpful learning tool. You can see the player execute and then imitate his actions. If you don't understand *why* he made the play that way, however, the learning experience is not complete. Understanding *why* helps actions become second nature on the field. If you don't understand why a big league player reacts a certain way in a specific situation, you will always have to draw on the image of that player making the play instead of quickly thinking the play through and reacting.

Football is a good analogy to use here. A wide receiver can know that a play is often called against a specific type of defense and that he's supposed to run ten yards and then cut straight across the middle. If the receiver knows why that play is run against that particular defense—that there are certain soft spots that are going to be open in the middle of the coverage—then he can make natural adjustments if his route is blocked. The receiver who just runs the pattern the way it's drawn up without understanding the spirit behind the play is much easier to cover. He gets to a certain point and isn't open and then has to figure out why he's covered. That split second of hesitation can result in an incomplete pass or even an interception.

Young children always ask, "Why?" That's because of their innate desire to learn. They have a thirst for knowledge that needs to be quenched. We encourage that at our camps. If you don't fully understand *why* as a coach, you're presented with a learning opportunity of your own. That's when you need to analyze the lesson and try to figure out why the skill is taught that way. Why do you field a ground ball with a wide base and your butt down? Because that pushes your hands out in front into the proper fielding position. If you can't figure out *why*, then you need to engage in debate with other coaches and instructors to see if there's an explanation that makes sense. If you can't explain the why, and you don't attempt to figure out the why and communicate it to your players, then you aren't teaching. You lose credibility, and the lesson is less likely to be accepted by the young player and practiced religiously. All the young player needs to know is that there's a reason for doing something. Then, more times than not, the player will accept the teaching and do his or her best to perform the task as directed.

CELEBRATE THE INDIVIDUAL

No two players are identical. They can differ in size, strength, speed, quickness, level of understanding, and so on. Each young player develops a certain style that he or she is comfortable with. It's our responsibility as parents, coaches, and instructors to use that style to enhance the player's skills.

We're all different. Each one of us has a different combination of talents. Some people are naturally stronger than others. Others are born faster. Some of us are gifted with extraordinary eye-hand coordination, while others have to work to develop that skill. It's imperative that youth coaches not lose sight of the innate physical differences in their players when teaching. Explaining basic fundamental skills—and why it's necessary to develop those skills—is important. But it's of equal importance to allow players to operate within their own comfort zones while applying those fundamentals to their skill sets. You can't clone one player to complete a task exactly the same way as another. Many instructors try to do this to an extreme, in the process overlooking another method that might make a player more successful because of that player's natural abilities.

Hitting instruction is a prime example. Everyone's talent and level of comfort in the batter's box varies. There are some key fundamental approaches that every hitter must take, but there are other components of a particular hitter's approach that may be drastically different from what most—or even all—other hitters do. A young hitter must feel as comfortable as possible in the batter's box. You can't force a young player into actions that are not natural. If he or she hits the ball hard consistently, I would argue that nothing should be changed. It is a hitter's job to go up to home plate and hit the ball hard. If that is happening consistently, don't tinker! The time for the teaching to begin is when a player is not making hard contact consistently.

One of the great things about American society is that everyone is different in so many ways. That is accepted and, in fact, it's celebrated and should not be overlooked in the world of sports. That's why Bill and I came up with "celebrate the individual." That little catchphrase also means "respect each individual and the talents he or she possesses." Young players are more apt to learn if they have more flexibility and freedom. They also bring more flair to the sport when you allow them to show what they're capable of achieving by using their own individual abilities. Part of the joy of being a kid is experimenting, trying new approaches and seeing how they work. As kids, how many of us went into the backyard, picked up a plastic bat, and pretended to be our favorite big league star—Ted Williams, Mickey Mantle, Willie Mays, Frank Robinson, or Brooks Robinson? Sometimes their stances worked and sometimes they didn't. But it was fun—and enlightening—to try.

Not everyone, especially young players, is going to hit or field exactly the same way. That should be viewed as a positive, both on and off the field. Even within the covers of this book it's a positive. Bill and I each have our own space—Cal's Corner and Bill's Ball Game—where we provide insights based on our own personal views and experiences. There's no one absolute right way to do anything in baseball. What makes the game great is that there are endless opinions and concepts that can be debated over and over. As a coach, make sure you appreciate everyone's natural abilities and challenge yourself to learn as much about the game as possible so that you can help adapt the necessary fundamental teachings to each young player's existing talents and comfort zone.

MAKE IT FUN

Baseball gets serious enough quickly enough. The one complaint you hear from kids who stop playing baseball is that the sport isn't exciting enough. For coaches the challenge is to make the game fun—even in practice situations. Of course, it's important not to overlook the fact that competitive situations such as games and contests are what excite young players the most.

Many times, usually in old baseball movies, you hear someone say that baseball is a simple game—you throw the ball, hit the ball, and catch the ball. However, baseball can be a very complicated game. The experience can get way too serious way too fast, especially in this day and age of travel teams and national youth tournaments. With young players, it's important to set aside time for teaching fundamentals, but coaches also must develop an understanding of the players' learning capacities and attention spans.

Learning is more likely to take place in a fun environment. That doesn't mean a coach should just lay out the balls and bats, choose up sides, and let the kids have at it. Drills can be structured so that they're fun. Contests can be used to emphasize the fundamentals on which drills focus. If young players are having fun, learning capacities and attention spans become less of a factor. The players are learning and not even realizing it. As far as they're concerned, they're having fun and will want to continue doing what they're doing. This allows for the repetition necessary to develop a solid fundamental base. In baseball, repetition and practice are the keys to success. But repetition and practice are two concepts that turn kids off and make the game seem like it's work. If you make drills fun, it's possible to excite young players about the game and give them the repetition necessary to become better players. When kids enjoy—and excel at—something, they generally stick with it. Mission accomplished!

Our objective is to show kids why baseball is so much fun. This is most important in the youngest age group—ages five to eight. However, it's important to keep the game fun even as players get older and become more serious. With the youngest group, you're introducing them to something that's new and different. They just want to have fun, so the teaching that goes on at this level should not follow traditional patterns of baseball instruction. As a coach you're always looking for short windows—maybe five seconds—in which you can teach, but it's best to try to be creative and think like a kid. What makes kids yell, scream, and smile? If you can think of methods that elicit that response and at the same time develop the basic motor skills necessary to play baseball, the experience will be unforgettable for you, the players, and the parents.

Games are always a hit with young players. Whether it's a scrimmage at the end of practice or skills contests that involve hitting, throwing, and eye-hand coordination, kids love the idea of testing themselves against others. Even at a young age, competition is fun. In fact, competition becomes more tense and stressful as age increases. As a coach, it's your responsibility to create an atmosphere of fun, excitement, and success. To accomplish this, it's important to be in tune with each player's skill level. If you ask every player to go up to home plate and take five swings and only a few of the players hit the ball consistently, is that fun? For the ones who can hit it is, but the others will get bored, frustrated, or upset. Be willing to move closer for some players or throw more softly. Learn the plane of each player's swing and try to toss the ball to that location so that he or she is more likely to hit the ball.

As a coach, do whatever it takes to allow all your players to experience success. When the players are successful, be animated. Yell, scream, and give out high-fives. Be a kid. If you're excited, they'll be excited. Small successes and positive reinforcement will keep young players coming back. If they come back, their motor skills will develop to the point where success will come more easily and more often. Some fun practice ideas can be found in the sections entitled "Fun Factor" that are located throughout this book.

Fun on the baseball field should not be limited to the youngest age group. The biggest challenge for coaches as the players get older is to continue thinking creatively about ways to keep the kids enthused about the game. Again, we believe in shorter, well-structured practices with small groups of players rotating to different drill stations every fifteen or twenty minutes. Keep the kids active and moving. Incorporate contests to work on the fundamentals that are being taught. The worst thing you can do as a coach is to have one player hitting and fourteen players shagging balls. And don't forget that all young players love to hit, and, most of all, they love to *play* baseball. Practice games and situational drills can give the players the feeling of being in a game while allowing coaches a tremendous forum in which to teach. Remember, it's easier to teach when the players are having fun.

In keeping with the philosophy behind the Ripken Way, when Bill and I started to put together our core staff of instructors for Ripken Baseball, all of whom made valuable contributions to the lessons in this book, we agreed that they had to meet certain requirements. The instructors would have to be former teammates of ours, and they would have to have a connection to Cal Sr. In short, they would have to be people who believe in our system of teaching. These six men have been valuable members of our team for many years:

Mike Boddicker

Mike is a former major league 20-game winner who once held the record for most strikeouts in an American League Championship Series game. He pitched in the big leagues for 14 years, winning 134 games and compiling a 3.80 ERA. His best season came in 1984 for Baltimore when he posted a 20–11 mark and a 2.79 ERA and earned a trip to the All-Star Game. Mike won the 1983 ALCS MVP award after striking out 14 Chicago White Sox in one game, and he was fourth in the 1984 American League Cy Young Award voting. He led the AL in ERA in 1984 and was second in 1983. Mike went on to play with the Boston Red Sox, Kansas City Royals, and Milwaukee Brewers before retiring in 1993. He was elected to the Baltimore Orioles Hall of Fame in August 2002.

Matt Cimo

Matt played professional baseball for nine years. He was a teammate of Bill Ripken's in the Orioles' organization and played in the San Francisco Giants', Chicago Cubs', and Philadelphia Phillies' organizations after graduating from Eastern Illinois University. An outfielder, Matt was named to the 1982 Rookie League All-Star team as a member of the Great Falls Giants, and he led the Class-A Clinton Giants in home runs in 1983. He hit .306 with 18 home runs and 64 RBIs for Double A Charlotte in 1987, earning a promotion to Triple A Rochester for the 1988 season. Rochester won the International League championship that year before falling to Indianapolis in the Triple A World Series. Matt currently serves as the head coach at Auburn High School in Alabama.

Ken Gerhart

Ken was one of the Orioles' most heralded minor league prospects of the 1980s after being selected in the fifth round of the 1982 amateur draft out of Middle Tennessee State University. He came up through the Baltimore organization at the same time as Bill Ripken and John Habyan, landing a spot on the big league roster in 1986. Ken remained with the Orioles until 1988 before being traded to the San Francisco Giants. A solid defensive outfielder who was blessed with power and tremendous speed, he belted 14 home runs while stealing nine bases in just 92 games for the Orioles in 1987. Ken recently was inducted into the MTSU Athletics Hall of Fame.

John Habyan

John broke into the big leagues with the Orioles in 1985 after coming up through the organization with Bill. He went on to pitch for the New York Yankees, Kansas City Royals, St. Louis Cardinals, California Angels, and Colorado Rockies during a successful 11-year major league career. In those 11 seasons he compiled an impressive 3.85 ERA and posted a 26-24 record with 12 saves.

Joe Orsulak

Joe began his major league career in 1983 with the Pittsburgh Pirates. The New Jersey native played for 14 seasons on five teams, the Pirates, Orioles, New York Mets, Florida Marlins, and Montreal Expos. In his 14 seasons Joe compiled a .273 average, 405 RBIs, and 57 home runs. He ended his big league playing career in 1997.

Mark Parent

Over the course of his impressive 13-year major league career, Mark caught for several big league clubs: the Orioles, Philadelphia Phillies, San Diego Padres, Detroit Tigers, Pittsburgh Pirates, Texas Rangers, and Chicago Cubs. In 1995 he hit a career-high 18 home runs in 81 games. His career .990 fielding percentage is the same as that of Ivan Rodriguez and better than that of Hall of Famer Johnny Bench (.987), considered to be two of the greatest catchers of all time. Most recently, Mark managed the Lancaster JetHawks, a Class A affiliate of the Seattle Mariners.

Our team has a great challenge before us: to take our philosophy further, through the camps and clinics operated by Ripken Baseball, as well as through Cal Ripken Baseball, the twelve-and-under division of Babe Ruth Baseball. That age division has about 700,000 players and is growing rapidly worldwide. We think this book will help, and we hope you enjoy it and find it a valuable resource. For more information, we invite you to visit ripkenbaseball.com and baberuthleague.org.

AT THE PLATE

The Fundamentals of Hitting

FIRST THINGS FIRST

By Cal Ripken, Jr.

Among Bill, Dad, and myself we have almost ninety years of experience in professional baseball. During these years I'll bet we've heard thousands of theories on hitting. That's a good thing and a bad thing. The good part is that these theories usually originate from some degree of success. A player has gone from having the natural ability to hit a baseball to applying some sort of teaching to it and combining that with learning through his own experience of hitting, which then produces results, and ultimately a theory or perspective on how he did it. I think this is good because it goes along with the idea that we're all made differently and there's more than one way of doing things. In short, it really does celebrate us as individuals. The bad part is that there are so many theories out there that it becomes confusing when you're trying to learn. We think that when you try to teach or learn hitting, there are a few things you should accept philosophically right from the start:

- Hitting a baseball takes a natural genetic ability. You can call this hand-eye coordination or just plain physical talent, but you must accept that a certain natural ability is required.
- There's more than one way to hit. In our camps we ask all the kids, "Can you name two players in the big leagues who hit exactly the same way?" The answer is no.
- There are basic fundamentals that will help any hitter, but it's necessary to mold those fundamentals to your individual talent.
- Repetitive practice is essential. You'll never hit unless you swing the bat, and we recommend swinging it over and over again.

These points are important because they open your mind and allow you to customize the task of hitting a baseball.

We believe very strongly that even though all hitters hit differently, there are some basic fundamentals that are common to each of them. We've tried to identify and simplify these fundamentals in this book. As you've probably noticed, hitting can be presented in a very complicated way. If you use all the baseball jargon and dissect every moving part, it can come off sounding like a foreign language. We have the ability and experience to filter out the overly technical, overly advanced, and downright overly analytical methods of teaching hitting. In a sense we've collected all the information about hitting, processed it, and reduced it to a simpler form. The idea is to build a base for hitting—your base—and have you build upon that base with practice and game experience, so that someday you can have enough success to join in and add to these theories yourself.

Remember: Hitting a baseball is difficult. Trying to hit a baseball can be frustrating. Hitting a baseball can also be one of the greatest feelings on earth. So please, never forget the joy of hitting a baseball. If you're learning, let this feeling motivate you through difficulties and practice. If you're teaching, let that feeling guide you to be more supportive and remind you to give everyone the chance to hit.

The Ripken Way of teaching is to simplify the message. This especially goes for hitting, but don't make the mistake of thinking that simple means superficial. As you build your own base of hitting with our simple fundamentals you'll discover many of the challenges and complexities of hitting. As you progress and your hitting becomes more advanced, we plan on being there offering advice in our camps and in the form of other books that will match your level. No matter what level you achieve, the secret of success will always be in the base of your fundamentals. We hope you benefit from our fundamentals and we hope you enjoy building your base for successful hitting.

DAD'S DESCRIPTION OF THE IDEAL HITTER

While putting this book together we looked through some of Dad's old baseball manuals and found this description of the ideal hitter that dates back forty years:

> That hitter would be one who would have a combination of these qualities: strength, determination, coordination, confidence, vision, rhythm, style, body control, quick hands, and the will to learn and to take advice. This hitter also would have a relaxed body and a loose, natural arm action. The hitter would blend the important parts of hitting—bat and grip, stance, stride, swing and follow-through—into a smooth, graceful motion. While waiting for the pitch, he would be perfectly relaxed with his feet spread comfortably. Eyes, hips, and shoulders would be level, and the weight of his body would be distributed almost evenly on both feet. The bat would be back and ready. He would watch the ball until it hits his bat. The swing would be a clean, free, crisp swing, and the ball would be struck out in front of the plate with the full power of the shifting weight behind it. His body would follow through in the direction the ball is hit, and his bat would continue under its own momentum to the rear of his body. At no stage of his swing would the batter's head jerk out of line. He would follow the course of the ball from the moment it left the pitcher's hand until it has hit the bat and is on its way.

As you can see, forty years later, the principles still apply.

CHOOSING THE RIGHT BAT

A bat is very much a matter of personal preference. It's all about what feels good to you as the hitter. Some people like thin handles and some like thick. Others like big barrels and others like small. Choosing the size of the bat is also a personal preference. Feel free to experiment, but be careful not to choose a bat that's way too heavy. If you do, your swing can become long and slow; the ideal swing is short and compact. Choosing a bat is a matter of trial and error. A good guide in determining if a bat is too heavy is to simply swing it and see if the bat controls the player or the player controls the bat. If the bat swings around and the player has trouble keeping his balance, it's too big. Control is important, not size or weight. Alex Rodriguez, for example, uses a 31-ounce bat, which is one of the lightest bats big league hitters use.

A lot of young hitters want to get a big, heavy bat, but as far as bat speed is concerned, a lighter aluminum bat is not a bad thing. An aluminum bat is stronger and lighter, so kids can start to mold their quicker swings earlier with a bat that they can actually swing. Years ago there were fewer options with wood bats, and even the smallest wood bats still may have been too heavy. A lot of times kids would bail out in their swing or step in the bucket, because it's a matter of trying to lug a too-heavy bat through the strike zone. So a young player might start to develop some bad habits because of the size of the bat.

We encourage players to use a bat that they can swing and that will allow them to use their wrists. And that usually means a lighter bat. As a general rule, we feel that a lighter bat lends itself to developing a quicker, shorter swing. But sometimes a hitter will pick up a bat and have success with it even though the bat's so big that it almost looks like a mismatch. In the end it all comes down to a hitter's comfort level.

It's a competitive and psychological advantage to use an aluminum bat, especially when everyone else is using one. But we also encourage players in their practice sessions or summer leagues to try a wood bat, because if a player has any aspirations of taking it on to the big leagues, he's going to have to transition from aluminum to wood at some point. We find that wood bats can be a good learning aid in practice. The sweet spot on a wood bat is much smaller than the sweet spot on an aluminum bat. You can hit the ball fat on an aluminum bat (fat means toward the label) and the ball will still jump off the bat pretty well. But if you hit the ball near the label with a wood bat, you're going to feel it in your hands and the ball is not going to jump off your bat. The bat might even break.

If you're trying to refine a hitter's point of contact, the wood bat can be a good teaching tool, and at some point you want a hitter to pick one up and see what it feels like. In order to enjoy the game nowadays, if you aren't going to the pros, you never have to transition. There's not much of an advantage at transitioning at a very young age. Either way your swing will develop and your talent will dictate what you do.

❖ ❖

CAL'S CORNER

Y ou might discover that a heavier bat gives a hitter the feeling that he has to get the bat started sooner. You can't swing a heavier bat by stepping straight forward with the same authority; you have to take it back a little bit (which is a good thing). That was the case with my son, Ryan, who's ten years old. Because Ryan has good strength in his arms and can really generate bat speed, if he picked up too light a bat he had a tendency to be way out in front. When I put a little heavier bat in his hands, he had to coil up to swing. He had much better results at that point, although his coach was telling him that his bat was too big because he was hitting the ball to the opposite field. But it was a matter of him waiting. I knew his swing would come around when he figured out how to pull the ball, and after a few games he did.

❖ ❖

THE GRIP

Once a hitter has chosen his bat, the next key element is the grip. The two important factors here are to hold the bat in your fingers and to grip it loosely in your hands. The bat shouldn't be jammed back in the rear of your hands. You should be able to align the middle knuckles (we call them the door-knocking knuckles) of both hands. Lining up the fat knuckles reduces bat speed and hinders your ability to move the bat through the hitting zone. What it really does is lock your wrists. We swing the bat with our forearms, our wrists, and our hands, and the right grip allows us to use all of them. When you're taking batting practice or you're at a camp with

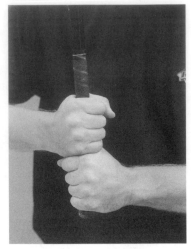

Hold the bat with a loose grip in the fingers. This will help promote a quick swing.

⊘ Lining up these knuckles will make it difficult to have a fluid swing.

a lot of hitting stations, loose hands are very, very important. And remember not to start out squeezing the bat too tight; tense muscles also slow your swing.

The grip is the single biggest problem we see for players age twelve and under, especially from age ten down. Coaches can introduce it in the five-to-eight age range, but it's one of the biggest things you have to repeat over and over again: Have young players understand the value of the grip.

Problems can occur with the grip when you don't get to a player early enough. We sometimes see sixteen-year-olds who have already developed some habits. Some of them could be good habits, but a lot of them could be bad habits. It's difficult to change a hitter's grip if he has had any kind of success with it. You know you can help him, but he's already developed another way of doing things. It's much harder to get that point across to an older kid than it is to the younger ones first picking up a bat.

Now, have there been people who played in the big leagues who hit with other grips? Absolutely. There are two extremes: One that comes to mind who really chokes the bat and lines up his knuckles in a different way is Bret Boone. He really squeezes the heck out of the bat. His knuckles are in, not what we teach for a hitting position. But Bret Boone is an All-Star and is a heck of a lot stronger than a young player that we're teaching. With the right grip the bat head remains on a level plane all the way through the hitting zone; with the wrong grip the bat has to roll over, so your margin for error is greater.

Albert Belle went to the extreme on the other side and held the bat near the end of his fingers with his top hand. We can't teach a kid to do what Albert Belle did. Certainly Albert had as much success as anybody at swinging the bat. We try to give examples of current guys who do things a little bit differently, but on the whole, lining up the knuckles properly is how you get bat speed. Everyone who hits in the big leagues has some bat speed. So there are players who grip the bat differently, but when you're looking at the overall consistency in a base of teaching, good hitting starts with the right grip.

With the right grip your swing remains level. The point of contact can be anywhere along the plane of your swing. If your timing is thrown off a little bit and you're late on the pitch, you'll still make good contact and hit the ball well to the opposite field. You want to have relaxed wrists and relaxed hands when you swing the bat. Your grip will tighten up naturally as you swing; if not, the bat's going to fly out of your hands. You want that bat to come through nice and quick.

One of the biggest problems that we see is parents and young coaches who constantly tell hitters, "Get your back elbow up." It's a phrase that got into this game somehow, some way, but it doesn't do any good. The further you put your back elbow up, the further the bat goes back into your top hand, and it almost forces your knuckles into the wrong alignment. We would rather the emphasis be put on the proper grip—leave the back elbow alone.

⊘ *Raising your back elbow forces the bat deep into your top hand.*

◆ ◆

CAL'S CORNER

I'm finding out that the grip on the bat is a critical part for kids Ryan's age. Early on, when kids are five years old or so, it's difficult to talk about the grip. You can introduce it, but it's just a matter of them holding the bat for themselves, and sometimes they have to separate their hands to actually swing it. However players swing a bat early on, just let them go. I can start to see now how with Ryan's grip he sets his hands up to be able to swing the bat freely and loosely, and it unlocks his wrists and allows his hands and forearms to have more of an effect. So he has a more complete swing and he's not just swinging it with his arms.

A word of caution: When a coach or parent tells a kid, "Get your back elbow up!" it usually changes the grip to an unfavorable one. Focus more on the right grip and less on the back elbow.

◆ ◆ ◆ ◆ ◆ ◆ ◆ ◆ ◆ ◆ ◆ ◆ ◆ ◆ ◆ ◆ ◆ ◆ ◆ ◆

THE STANCE

Just as a hitter should select a bat that's comfortable, he should also use a batting stance that's comfortable. Usually that would be a stance just as if we were standing and talking. Your feet should be shoulder-width apart or slightly wider, with your weight balanced. There are many types of batting stances—closed stances, open stances, crouched stances, modified stances, and so on. This is something Cal is famous for because he had about a thousand of them.

As we said up front, we want to celebrate each player's individuality. We want every hitter to have a good, balanced, workable stance. We tell young players to be comfortable, feel positive, and make it work for you. Remember, the stance is just a starting position. Nothing has happened yet. The pitcher hasn't thrown the ball. You haven't begun to swing the bat yet. The key to being able to hit is to be comfortable and relaxed. But whether it's open or closed, straight up or crouched, there are three essential elements to a good stance:

◆ **Balance.** Good balance will provide you with a stable, athletic base. A stable, athletic base is a starting point for all of your movements on a baseball field. You're going to have to do something with that bat in your hands: You're going to have to gather your energy and swing it, so you're going to want to swing it from a solid base. Your stance provides you with that base. Some people's base is open, which means that their front foot is further from home plate than their back foot. Some

Your stance should be balanced and comfortable.

people's base is closed, which is the other way around. At our camps we generally don't have a problem with anybody's stance, provided it works, and provided it gives them balance and stability.

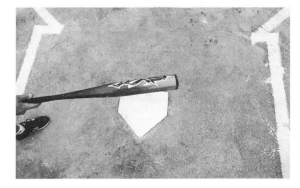

The plate is the reference point for the strike zone. You have to be able to cover the entire plate with your bat.

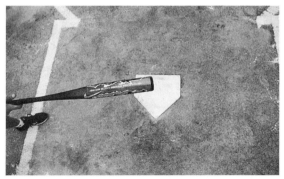

⊘ If you have poor plate coverage like this, you'll have trouble hitting a pitch on the outside corner.

◆ **Plate coverage.** The plate is the reference point for the strike zone. The pitcher is trying to use the whole strike zone, so the hitter has to be in a position to cover that zone. That plate doesn't seem so big, but believe us, sometimes the interpretation of the strike zone varies with the umpire. You have to be able to cover the entire plate with your bat—that's simply called plate coverage. You have to be in a position where you can hit a pitch on the outside corner, but also be able to handle something inside. Ideally you want to get the head of the bat to the baseball over the plate.

◆ **Being in a position to see the ball.** You'll hear that you need to see the ball with both eyes. You'll hear that one eye is your dominant eye. These things are true, but just remember that you can't hit what you don't see. Obviously it's critical that your stance provides you with the ability to pick up the baseball. At the big league level you're talking about the pitcher being 60 feet, 6 inches away from you, and the guy is throwing 95 miles per hour. The ball gets there so quickly, and you need to be able to pick it up. If you have a stance that's extreme and closed and you can't see well, then that's not a good stance.

⊘ If your stance is too closed, it makes it difficult to pick up the baseball.

CAL'S CORNER

A simple way to determine if you have good plate coverage is the drop-bat method. When you're standing at the plate, hold the bat out as if you're swinging, right over home plate, at the point where you would be making contact, and then simply drop the bat. It gives you a reference. The plate's right there and when you drop the bat, you'll see if you have home plate covered. Another way to check is to have a teammate stand in front of you or behind you as you swing the bat and give you an idea if your bat is covering the plate.

Startng your hands near the back shoulder can eliminate some wasted movement.

BAT PLACEMENT

Okay, you have your grip and your stance, and now you're getting ready to hit. You need a starting position for your hands and bat. This is what we call bat placement. The placement of the bat on or off the shoulder is a matter of personal comfort and should be left up to the individual hitter. You just want to place the bat in a position where you can fire it, or swing it, quickly. Getting the bat head to the ball is the most important thing.

The position we recommend is this: Get your hands at approximately the top of the strike zone and hold the bat at about a 45-degree angle. Your hands should start near your back shoulder in a comfortable position; that's where the swing starts. Your hands are basically at the top of the strike zone. We like you to feel that your swing will be down and to the baseball. And remember to swing through the baseball.

BILL'S BALL GAME

You might say, "I see big league hitters on TV holding their hands in all sorts of different positions before they swing." You're right, but if you watch closely when the pitch is delivered, you'll notice that no matter where a big leaguer starts his hands, he always gets them to the firing area as the ball is being delivered. So when teaching young players, we feel that it's easier to just have them start their hands there.

THE WEIGHT SHIFT

It's important to have your body and swing go together. The weight shift helps keep everything together. The weight shift simply means that you're going to take your weight from a balanced, stable, athletic position and you're going to gather that energy, take your weight to the back side, and then bring it forward. Just like a cobra you might see on the Discovery Channel that coils back and gathers all his energy for a quick, fast strike, a hitter gathers his energy and then takes that energy forward to swing the bat. At our camps we like to use the expression "You have to go back to go forward." It sounds backward, but people remember it pretty well because it makes you think, What does that mean? What it means is that you start in a balanced position before transferring your weight first to your back side and then to your front side as you stride into the swing. You want all your energy to come together at one time. A hitting tee is an excellent way to practice the weight shift: The ball is just sitting there so you never have to rush. You can develop a rhythm. Work toward a level of consistency, trying to do it the same way every time.

We like to use the tee drill to work on weight shift: Go back to go forward.

THE PITCHER'S RELEASE POINT

There are many different release points. Some pitchers throw from over the top. Some throw from a three-quarter arm slot. Some throw sidearm. A hitter has such a short period of time to see the ball after it leaves the pitcher's hand. You have to be able to see the ball. And it's critical to see it at its earliest point.

At the highest level we have the ability to see pitchers over and over again. We can watch them on TV, we can watch them warm up, and we can get a good idea of where each guy's release point is to give us a little edge. You don't have quite that same advantage on the youth level, but the concept is still the same. You still want to pick up the ball as early as possible, and the best way to do that is to figure out where the pitcher's release point is and focus on that spot. That doesn't mean you want to stare at that spot, because if you stare at something too long you don't see it clearly. You want to get in the box and get relaxed, and then, as the pitcher gets ready to deliver, that's when your focus starts to come into play. Before the pitcher throws the ball you might look down at his feet, look at his chest, look at the bird on the front of his cap—but when he gets ready to throw, that's when you want to turn your eyes to his release point. If you look at the release point too early, you're going to end up staring and you're only going to see a blur.

THE STRIDE

As with the stance, the stride varies to a certain extent with each individual. Most hitters have a short stride, other hitters have a longer one. Some stride a bit toward home plate, others stride a little away from the plate. The bottom line is what works for you as a hitter. But fundamentally there are two things about the stride that we feel are important:

◆ **The stride should be toward the pitcher.** The stride puts you in a position to strike the ball. By striding toward the pitcher your body position is good for both the inside pitch and the outside pitch.

A short, soft stride is preferable, with the front foot and lead shoulder going toward the pitcher. That helps create a fast, fluid swing.

◆ **A short, soft stride is preferable.** A short stride keeps your head on the same plane, allowing you to track the ball from the pitcher's hand to the bat. A shorter stride allows you to wait on the pitch longer, which prevents you from being fooled by pitches of different types and speeds.

◆ ◆

BILL'S BALL GAME

You want to talk about a guy who took a long stride? Watch video of Dave Winfield. He practically stepped on the pitcher. That's how far he took his stride. Jeff Bagwell, on the other hand—his stride backs up. Paul Molitor sometimes didn't stride at all. But these are three extreme cases on stride. Dave Winfield and Paul Molitor had great careers. Jeff Bagwell can flat-out hit. But we can't teach what they do. Their strides are individual to them. The reason we teach a short stride is plain and simple, though: The shorter the stride and the softer the stride, the less the head moves. When your head doesn't move, your eyes don't move, and when your eyes don't move, you see the ball better.

◆ ◆

THE SWING

When you swing the bat, you want to take a short, direct path to the ball. Your front arm is the one that provides that short path. We encourage a quick, level swing, one that utilizes the forearms, hands, and wrists.

Don't overanalyze your particular swing. Your strength and sense of timing will take over. You'll develop your swing by swinging, but remember, it's all about the hitter getting into the proper position to start with.

The point of contact is generally going to be out in front of home plate. This allows for good extension, and it also allows for more bat speed. If you hit the ball too far back, your swing essentially has been cut in half and you have less time and space to generate full bat speed. Conversely, if you hit the ball too far out in front, your swing is in the slowing-down mode when contact is made. There are optimum points of contact for everyone, and they vary for each individual. The key is to find your best point of contact. Contact on the bat head is first and foremost. You want to focus on getting the bat head to the ball.

The swing should start with the hitter's hands in the ready position, which is approximately at the top of the back shoulder. The ideal swing is level. You'll hear coaches say things like "Stay on top of the ball," or "Swing down on the ball." They're just communicating a feeling. In order to swing level it feels like we're swinging down or staying on top, but actually we're swinging level.

Sometimes coaches use those expressions to correct a hitch. When a hitter has a hitch in his swing, it simply means he's dropping his hands below his shoulder at the start of his swing.

We sometimes see young hitters who are trying to get the ball in the air or trying to put more power into it, and they end up pulling off the ball.

⊘ *A hitch—dropping the hands below the shoulder—could lead to problems with your swing.*

They start their forward motion too soon. Remember, the weight shift goes back first. When we try to hit the ball in the air or try to hit it too far, our bodies have a tendency to get out in front. Our hands never get into the hitting position, and a common symptom occurs. You must pull your front shoulder to try to get to the ball. The reason we bring this up here in the swing section is to make the point that your swing is affected by your body position. Sometimes we try to fix the swing when we should be focusing on your body position. Put your body in a good hitting position and your swing will take care of itself.

You have to keep your front shoulder in, or closed. If your front shoulder stays in longer and goes toward the pitcher with your stride, you have a better chance of hitting than when your front shoulder starts to leave, or open, early. When that happens, your swing slows down, your bat loops, and the result is that you get a lot of fly balls to the opposite field because you're most likely not getting the bat head to the ball.

◆ ◆

BILL'S BALL GAME

I remember when I was playing in the minor leagues I'd sometimes call Dad and say, "I had two at-bats last night where I had balls that I should've been hitting hard and instead I hit some lazy fly balls to right field." And Dad would say, "It sounds to me like you're pulling off a little bit or you're flying open with your front shoulder." That slows the bat down and drags it through the zone, and you end up hitting a weak fly ball to right field. "So tomorrow in batting practice," he'd say, "I want you to concentrate on keeping your front shoulder in a little longer and trying to hit the ball back up the middle." Remember the importance of your front shoulder. It's important in hitting, and it's important in throwing. And that's still a basic point that we teach.

◆ ◆

CAL'S CORNER

Visualize the swing this way: You're standing at home plate, and your shoulders are squared against the plate. If you draw a line between your right shoulder and your left shoulder, it should be pointing right to the pitcher. As you're getting ready to hit, as you get ready to load, or take your energy back as the first part of your weight shift, your front shoulder should turn slightly in toward the plate. This is a difficult thing for some kids to grasp, especially the ten-and-under age group. I've had some success communicating this point by referring to the number on the back of the kids' jerseys. I simply say that when they're loading, or going back, they should try to show the pitcher their number on the back of their jersey. Of course they can't fully turn their back to the pitcher and still see the pitch, but they understand the concept. As coaches we just need to make sure they don't turn in too far.

◆ ◆ ◆ ◆ ◆ ◆ ◆ ◆ ◆ ◆ ◆ ◆ ◆ ◆ ◆ ◆ ◆ ◆ ◆

◆ ◆ ◆ ◆ ◆ ◆ ◆ ◆ ◆ ◆ ◆ ◆ ◆ ◆ ◆ ◆ ◆ ◆ ◆

BILL'S BALL GAME

You'll often hear people talk about hitting an outside pitch to the opposite field (right field for a righthanded hitter). That's not always the case. Your swing and your timing will determine which direction the ball goes. But if your approach is sound and your swing is sound, the outside pitch doesn't necessarily have to go to the opposite field. It's okay to hit that outside pitch right back at the pitcher, or even to pull it. Your approach should be the same for every pitch: Stay on the baseball with your eyes and front shoulder and concentrate on hitting the ball hard.

◆ ◆ ◆ ◆ ◆ ◆ ◆ ◆ ◆ ◆ ◆ ◆ ◆ ◆ ◆ ◆ ◆ ◆ ◆

BILL'S BALL GAME

The location of the pitch will usually determine where your best point of contact is. The general rule—make contact a little bit out in front of home plate—most applies for a pitch over the middle of the plate. An outside pitch is best hit a little further back. On an inside pitch you want to make contact further out in front.

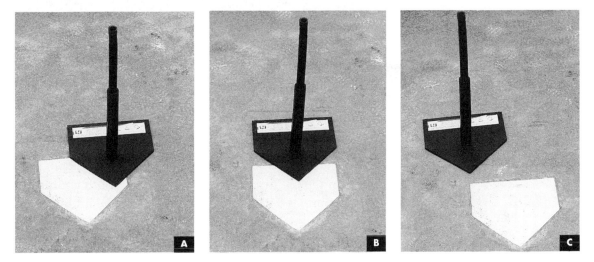

Here the batting tee marks three good points of contact. Contact should be made out in front. Generally speaking, you should let the pitch away travel longer (A), the inside pitch you'll hit more out front (C), and the pitch down the middle you'll hit somewhere in between (B).

THE FOLLOW-THROUGH

The key to the follow-through is swinging *through the baseball.* If you don't follow through properly, you're essentially slowing your bat down at the point of contact. We want maximum bat speed at the point of contact, and a good follow-through is a result of that. The follow-through is a product of the momentum generated by your bat speed. If your swing mechanics are correct, the follow-through will take care of itself. It's not something you should have to think about. A good follow-through should come naturally.

On the left is a two-handed follow-through and on the right is a one-handed follow-through. Both are okay.

There are basically two ways to follow through: keeping two hands on the bat or releasing the top hand. Both are fine, as long as your bat doesn't slow down through the hitting zone.

◆ ◆

CAL'S CORNER

Most coaches say that it's much easier to try switch-hitting early and get a player used to it, just like anything else in the game. That's true: The earlier you try it, the easier it is to get accustomed to it. Eddie Murray, my longtime teammate, comes to mind as an exception. Eddie was in Double A and was struggling a little bit, although he had a lot of talent hitting righthanded. It was then that he decided to try switch-hitting, and Dad had an influence in making him into a switch-hitter. That's a rare case—someone who can pick up switch-hitting late in his career, especially a professional ballplayer in Double A, and go on to hit 500 home runs.

I would recommend that a coach look at a player and judge for himself if that player has an aptitude to do it. A couple of teammates of my son, Ryan, are switch-hitting, but I know that Ryan's left hand is dominant. I knew it from the first minute he picked up a ball. I tried to encourage him to use the opposite side in basketball and some other sports to develop some coordination, but he just doesn't have the ability to turn the bat around to the other side and swing righthanded. It was obvious to me when I played, too, so I didn't even consider switch-hitting. But if you have someone who seems to have pretty good aptitude both ways, I'd encourage it. You'll have plenty of time at different stages of development to shelve it if the production isn't there, but we really shouldn't be paying too close attention to overall statistics at the youth levels. We just want to see that the players are learning the game and improving, and they should have the opportunity to see if they can hit from the other side. It's a confidence thing, too. If a hitter can stand in the batter's box and, no matter if the guy's throwing hard righthanded or if a lefthander comes in, he feels like he has a chance to get a hit, that's a big advantage.

◆ ◆

BUNTING

As with other baseball skills, there's not one perfect way to bunt. What we try to do at our camps is give the players some basic fundamental guidelines on bunting and explain the reasons why.

From your normal stance, simply pivot on both feet and slightly bend your knees. If you have an upright stance or if your feet are close together, spread your feet to about shoulder-width apart. A good base and balance are important in bunting.

We don't recommend squaring both feet to the pitcher, though many hitters have used this method effectively. We believe that this puts the batter in a vulnerable position. If the ball should get away from the pitcher, the hitter is not in a good position to get out of the way. This position also locks you into a bunt-only mode. If you wanted to swing or try a slash bunt, you'd have to step back into a more normal hitting stance.

When bunting, keep the barrel of the bat above the hands and the bat out in front of home plate.

⊘ *Allowing the barrel of the bat to drop below the hands is a bunting no-no (left). Squaring around (right) can leave you vulnerable to the pitch.*

Point the bat head at the pitcher and transfer your weight to your front foot. This gets the bat out front, so you can see the ball hit the bat. The bat should now be in fair territory.

Slide the top hand up on the bat to about the label. Grip the bat between your thumb and index finger. Don't let the bat slip back into your hand. The space in between the bat and your hand will give, much like a shock absorber, and will soften the impact of the ball off the bat.

Hold the bat at the top of the strike zone. Bend your knees to bunt the lower pitches. Don't attempt to bunt a pitch above your starting point.

The bat head should be above your hands when contact is made. Let the ball hit the bat. Don't stab at the ball. It has been said that you want to "catch" the ball with the bat, the same way you use your glove to catch the ball. This is a helpful comparison. The bottom hand guides the direction of the ball. You can move it like the rudder on a ship.

Don't worry about showing bunt too early. In a sacrifice bunt situation it's the quality of the bunt, not the element of surprise, that gets the job done. It's when you're bunting for a hit that the element of surprise becomes important.

◆ ◆

BILL'S BALL GAME

When we go through our drills, we want to make everything as close to a game situation as we can. As we said up front, perfect practice makes perfect. Whatever you do in practice is what you're going to do in a game situation. The same thing goes for all our hitting drills. Good pace with the drills provides good, realistic game-type action.

◆ ◆

PERFECT PRACTICE MAKES PERFECT: THE TEE DRILL

To execute this drill, the batter places the ball on the hitting tee, gets in a comfortable stance, focuses on the ball, gathers his energy with his weight shift, and swings. We use the hitting tee to teach the concept of weight shift because the ball sits right on that tee and never moves. Your timing can't be thrown off. Nobody's throwing you a pitch, so you don't have to worry about getting ready too fast. You can take all the time in the world to gather your energy and then decide when you want to take it forward to hit.

The tee is the best way to work on your weight shift and develop a rhythm to your swing. At our camps we always go around and ask the kids who are hitting off the tee, "What are

In the tee drill, don't be afraid to exaggerate the weight shift and swing with a purpose.

you working on at this station?" And they say, "I'm working on my weight shift. I'm going back to go forward." We want to stress that simple message and only that message for the guys who are hitting off the tee. We're not saying that you can't use the tee to have fun or to hit the ball to the opposite field or to teach other things, such as hitting the ball up the middle or pulling the ball, or hitting it out in front of the plate. But at our camps the tee is used primarily to get one message across: Go back to go forward. Cal encourages the kids to exaggerate their back movement, so they can fully get the feeling of having their weight on the back side and then transferring it to the front side. Most people think of the weight shift as a movement that goes forward, but the weight should start from a balanced position, go to the back side, and then transfer to the front side.

BILL'S BALL GAME: TEEING OFF ON THE TEE

I was watching the kids hit off the tee at one of our camps. They were concentrating on going back to go forward, and I took the bat and said, "Look, we have these nice nets in front of the balls on the tee. Go ahead and rip a hole in that net. Hit it hard." And I got in there and demonstrated. I really wound up on it and just unleashed and swung hard. They had a good time after I did that. It kind of woke them up a little bit. They were finessing the tee work too much. The purpose of this drill is to go back to go forward. But when you're hitting, we don't want you to just make contact—we want you to make *hard* contact. So think about weight shift, but when it's time to swing, swing like you mean it.

PERFECT PRACTICE MAKES PERFECT: THE SOFT-TOSS DRILL

As with the tee, many things can be accomplished with soft-toss, but once again we like to stress a very simple message: In this drill, we work on the components of the swing itself. The ideal swing is one that is short and quick to the baseball.

The important teaching concept to stress with the soft-toss drill is "loose hands, quick bat." So it's all about the grip in this drill. The hitter should grip the bat loosely in the fingers and concentrate on using the wrists and hands to swing it. Don't worry about body position or the hips or anything else. The focus should be on the hands and wrists.

The tosser is vital to the success of this drill. The tosses can come from in front (behind a protective screen) or from the side. The tosser can also throw to different locations. High

When doing the soft-toss drill, it's important for the feeder to toss strikes.

school players can toss to one another, but for the younger players a coach should be making the tosses. If the tosser is careful to consistently give the hitter good, hittable tosses, the hitter doesn't have to think, and he's better able to focus on the drill's main purpose: loose hands, quick bat.

◆ ◆

◆ ◆

PERFECT PRACTICE MAKES PERFECT: ONE-ARM DRILL

A slightly more advanced drill, but one that we've been able to use even with seven- and eight-year-olds, is the one-arm drill. The purpose of this drill is to create a direct path to the baseball with the lead arm.

A lot of coaches use the one-arm drill, and some will replace a little guy's bat and have him use a smaller one, which makes it easier because the bottom arm isn't that stable to swing the bat. But we would encourage you to use the same bat and do not trade out. Whatever bat you normally use, start out with your hand on the knob, in its normal position, and take the top hand away. The tosser is stationed out in front of the batter (on a stool or on one knee, behind a screen). Start out by swinging normally, with two hands, for the first five swings, just to get a point of reference for the spot from which the ball is being thrown. Then take the top hand off the bat and swing with just the one arm for five swings. This part will be difficult. Then finish by swinging with both hands again for five swings.

The batter should notice a shorter, more compact swing during the final set. Hitters may have problems with this drill—even a lot of big league hitters have trouble maintaining the stability of their bat in the one-armed hitting position. This is supposed to feel awkward, but the only way you'll be able to get the bat head to the ball with this lack of strength is to take it on a direct path.

If the hitters are having problems with this drill and it looks really awkward, tighten the hitting elbow down to their side. Don't say much the first time. Just say, "Take your hand off

To help you with the one-arm drill it's okay to choke up a little and tuck your elbow to your side. When executing this drill, the hitter should take the lead hand on a direct path to the baseball.

the bat and swing." Then you can say, "Tighten your elbow down to your side, which will give you stability and shorten it up a little bit." It'll be easier to start it from this position. Also, if the hitters continue to have problems, they can choke up a little bit. This gives them more stability holding the bat, so they can do something with it. But again, this drill is designed to be a little awkward. It's designed to send a message. Even if the hitters swing and miss five times, say, "Okay, two hands back on the bat."

If you can do ten as opposed to five and then return to ten or fifteen two-handed swings, then do that. But we always start our campers with two hands, then have them take a little brief session with one hand, and then come back to two hands to finish up so that they get a feel for what the bottom hand is doing. If you've never tried this drill, it makes your last five swings or your last ten swings come together in a way that's really hard to explain. But that's because your bottom hand is taking a little shorter, more direct route to the ball automatically. Some kids will be able to hit the ball with one arm and some will not have as much success, but by going through this drill the batter should notice a shorter, more compact swing during the final set.

◆ ◆

◆ ◆

PERFECT PRACTICE MAKES PERFECT: FREE HITTING

Once the other drills have been completed, we feel that it's time to let the players get in the batting cage and have some fun. We call this free hitting. Hitting is supposed to be the most fun part of the game, so as coaches the last thing we want to do is give a young player too much information when he's hitting. It's hard enough to hit when you're just reacting naturally to a pitched ball. When someone starts talking about hand positioning, weight shift, and other technical points during free hitting, the player may become confused or think too much and the fun may be taken out of hitting.

The time to work on all of those little details is during the drills that we've previously covered. Free hitting is the player's time to take everything that was learned during tee work, soft-toss, and the one-arm drill and put it all together. When the player gets in the cage to hit, a rhythm and timing should automatically develop from the drill work that has already been done. When you're at a camp, you've been moving from one station to another doing hitting drills, fifteen minutes at a time, taking your repetitions. But repetition is monotonous. Repetition is boring. When you finally get the freedom to come to the cage, the last thing you want is a coach sitting behind you saying, "Do this, do that," on every single swing. Coaches should give the kids the freedom just to hack, without even thinking. Don't overcoach when it comes to hitting. Be disciplined and strict on the drills for what they're designed to do, but then give some leeway when it comes to free hitting. Make note of any flaws and address them at another time during drill work.

◆ ◆ ◆ ◆ ◆ ◆ ◆ ◆ ◆ ◆ ◆ ◆ ◆ ◆ ◆ ◆ ◆ ◆ ◆

◆ ◆ ◆ ◆ ◆ ◆ ◆ ◆ ◆ ◆ ◆ ◆ ◆ ◆ ◆ ◆ ◆ ◆ ◆

CAL'S CORNER

When you're doing cage work, or hitting the ball into a net, you don't get a chance to gauge the distance of the ball, so young hitters have a tendency to stay within themselves and not try to overswing and hit the ball too far. We constantly preach to hit the ball hard somewhere—we don't care where it goes. We just want you to stay on the ball and hit it hard. But once you get to a big field, especially if you have a fence, sometimes kids are going to want to see how far they can hit the ball. I know my son, Ryan, anytime there's a chance to do it, especially the fence in right field, he starts to pull off and overswing. You still need to take batting practice out in the field, but with the cage work you have a chance to focus more on the makeup of the swing. There's less of a tendency to overswing when you're not worried about how far the ball will go.

It's still fun to hit the ball over the fence, though. So I'll sometimes encourage the players to take the tee outside the cage, and we'll combine outfield play with the hitting tee. I'll tell the kids to hit the ball out of centerfield. In order to hit the ball far, you have to take your weight back, gather your energy, and then come through, but you also have to be precise enough to hit the ball without pulling your head, because if you pull your head and your shoulders you're going to hit the tee or you're going to miss the ball completely. So there's some control and some containment of the kids' swings, and by swinging straight up the middle and trying to aim that way they're keeping all the balance points and their swings in line.

❖ ❖

❖ ❖

FUN FACTOR: CATCHER'S GEAR

Hitting can be very difficult, and young players can get frustrated. So we try to take the focus off the frustration and make it into something we can laugh about. We suggest that parents and coaches of young players try putting on full catcher's equipment and sitting on a stool at a close distance and pitching to the player. This drill is designed for the very youngest of players. When a player gets older, you should consider using foam balls for safety. Encourage the hitter to hit the ball back at you. First of all, from the kid's perspective, it just looks funny. Second, the hitting element is just part of a bigger game: Knock the funny-looking guy off the stool. Become animated when the ball comes near you or actually hits you. This adds to the fun.

With this game there are basic hitting fundamentals being taught while having a great time. The fundamentals are:
- staying on the ball
- not pulling off
- striding toward the pitcher
- going straight to the ball
- creating a short, compact swing
- not overswinging (unless they're trying to kill you!)
- swinging level
- hitting the ball back up the middle

❖ ❖

◆ ◆

FUN FACTOR: GOALIE GAME

If you have access to a tennis machine, this is another fun, creative game: In a gym, set up a hockey or lacrosse goal to serve as a backstop, and make a home plate right in front of the net. The tennis machine should be set up to shoot tennis balls as a pitching machine would, over home plate. It seems like hitting off a pitching machine, but the creative part of this game is in the presentation.

In this game we call the hitter "the goalie." The tennis machine is trying to score a "goal," and the job of the goalie is to keep the ball out of the net. But the only way the goalie can keep it out of the net is with the bat. This, of course, is batting practice disguised, but the focus has been shifted. Instead of a swing and a miss and the frustration of failure, the result is a "goal" and the game continues with the next pitch, or "shot." (There are other creative variations of this game that you can try, using plastic balls or sock balls, for example.)

This game hones the following skills:
- hand-eye coordination
- bat control
- a short swing with an emphasis on making contact
- not worrying about where the ball goes—hitting it where it's pitched

◆ ◆

THE HITTER'S CHECKLIST

- Select a bat you can handle.
- Keep your head still.
- Concentrate on solid, hard contact.
- Learn the strike zone, and hit strikes.
- Keep your front shoulder and chin tucked in.
- Keep your hands back.
- Hold the bat with a loose grip in the fingers. The fingers will tighten automatically when the swing takes place.
- Learn to hit your strength. Every hitter has a strength, just as every hitter has a weakness. Hit your pitch. When you get it, don't let it get away.
- Stay on the balls of your feet and balanced.
- Remember the concept of going back to go forward to generate weight shift.
- Take a short stride—a long stride will only throw you off-balance. Short and soft is what we're looking for.
- Make the pitcher come to you. Don't be anxious in going after him.
- Bat control is very important. If you're having trouble controlling the bat, try a smaller one or choke up.
- Stay on top and swing level. You should feel like you're swinging down on the ball.
- Remember to keep the front shoulder in. That allows you to get the bat head out in front and prevents dropping the back shoulder.

ON THE BASES

FIRST THINGS FIRST

By Cal Ripken, Jr.

When I was in the big leagues and it came time in spring training to review baserunning, everyone wanted to call in sick (and I'm not sure that's even allowed in baseball). At the major league level—and keep in mind this was just a review—this had to be one of the most boring things to do. It wasn't necessarily the subject matter, it was how it was presented.

Picture all of us in our uniforms huddled around Cal Sr. on the infield in the hot sun. Dad would take us through all of the responsibilities of a baserunner, starting from the on-deck circle. The talk would then move to the home plate area and right around the bases, one base at a time. Dad had gone through this ritual every year. But for him there was no other way; the field was his classroom. We would try to be good students, but listening to anyone talk for more than an hour when all we wanted to do was play was challenging.

It's amazing how much of those talks we retained, though. I'll bet Bill and I can recite those spring training lectures verbatim. We know that because a lot of writing this book involved taking what we have stored in our brains and putting it down on paper. The good news here is that an hour-long talk translates into a wealth of written pages. I'll bet at this stage of the game you're a little worried. You probably have the same apprehensions that we felt in spring training. But don't worry: We've edited the boring parts out and simplified the message (leaving in all the good stuff). We realize we can't overwhelm you or we run the risk of losing you. But rest assured that our baserunning section is thorough.

Baserunning is important. Just think about it: The goal of a baseball game is to score more runs than the other team. Baserunning is the means by which we do it. Granted, if we hit home runs all the time we don't have to worry about how to run the bases, but that's not going to happen. Just like hitting, fielding, and throwing, baserunning has certain fundamentals. These fundamentals, like all other fundamentals, should be applied to your individual talents.

The game has been played for a long, long time, and the distance between the bases hasn't changed. So that means there have been a lot of games played and a lot of runners running around those bases in all kinds of situations. Mistakes have been made and guidelines have developed. Dad might have been there to witness them all. We know that's not true, but after listening to him lecture on the subject we could make a good case.

Everyone runs the bases. Baserunning is certainly not just for the fast guys. The keys to good baserunning lie in your own instincts, knowledge of situations, and a good understanding of the principles and fundamentals. To be a good baserunner you have to learn to rely on your eyes and your own judgment rather than on the first- and third- base coaches. A good baserunner very rarely needs the coach. You'll discover that your instincts and your knowledge of the situations will grow as you play, but we'll get you started on building your fundamental base with our version of a trip around the bases.

ON-DECK RESPONSIBILITIES

Let's start by talking about your duties before you even get to the plate. No matter where you are on a baseball field you have to be heads-up and alert, and you always have a job to do. When you're in the on-deck circle you have more to do than just watch the pitcher and get ready to hit. You're the eyes for any baserunners who may be coming to the plate and trying to score. So when necessary you need to clear the bat, catcher's mask, and any other equipment from the sliding area and let that runner coming in from third base know if he needs to slide or if he can come in standing up. If he's sliding, then direct him away from the ball and the tag.

As the on-deck hitter you can also root for and encourage the hitter, and you can advise him to run on a third strike that has eluded the catcher.

APPROACHING THE BATTER'S BOX

The first thing to do as you go up to the plate to hit is pick up the third-base coach and look for the sign. Often the coach is ready to give that sign right away. If he's able to flash the sign early, it has less chance of being picked up by the other team.

Look to see how the defense is setting up. Are the corner infielders playing back, or are they in? Are they playing a shift? Are they holding any runners on? By checking the defense you're able to assess your options as a hitter.

AFTER CONTACT

As soon as you make contact, your time as a hitter is finished; you've become a baserunner. Start to run immediately. Don't watch the ball for too long. There's a brief moment when you need your eyes to pick up the ball to give you some important information. Is it a base hit? Possibly extra bases? Is it a ground ball? But don't get in the habit of watching the ball, because it only slows you down. There'll be many times when you're thrown out at first base by an eyelash, and that initial delay could be the difference between an out and a hit.

If you hit a ground ball to the infield, run a straight line to first base: a direct route from the point at which you've finished your swing right to the bag. Batters who hit a routine ground ball are usually upset. But instead of lagging to first or throwing the bat or yelling, you're better off taking out that aggression by running to first base as hard as you can.

Don't forget about the 45-foot rule. The rule states that within the last 45 feet (assuming 90-foot bases) you must be inside the designated area: either on the baseline or in foul territory.

Aim for the front part of the bag. That's the closest part to home plate, so it makes sense to touch the base there. Hit the base with either foot. The important thing is not to break stride. Stay in stride and eliminate stutter-stepping. Run through the base. Pretend the finish line is another 20 feet past the bag. That way you'll hit first base at full speed.

Avoid sliding into first base. Sliding doesn't get you there any faster, and you're subjecting yourself to possible injury. Sometimes it's useful and necessary when avoiding a tag at first base, but otherwise you should avoid it.

ON A BASE HIT

Leave home plate thinking double. We want our hitters to run until the defense stops them. Take a gradual line toward the first-base coaching box in preparation for the turn at first. Don't make a keyhole or question mark turn—a turn in which you go straight down the line and then make an arc halfway to first base. Touch the bag with either foot and try not to break stride.

When you hit the bag, you want to touch the front part of the base closest to home plate.

⊘ Stepping on the back side of the base makes it a longer distance.

When rounding first base, touch the base in the center of the edge facing second base, so you can push off.

⊘ *Don't touch the corner of the bag. You risk missing the base completely or turning an ankle.*

Use the base to help propel you to the next base. You can use it as a sort of starting block to push off. With the old-style bases the teaching was to touch the inside corner. The new bases give us the opportunity to use the base on the turn, and touching more of the middle of the base gives the umpire less chance to miss the call.

On a possible extra-base hit always pick up the ball with your eyes after rounding first base. While rounding first, listen for help from the first base coach.

◆ ◆

CAL'S CORNER

You don't have to be fast to be a good baserunner. The best baserunners rely on their instincts, their anticipation, and simply being prepared: knowing the situation in terms of the number of outs and how the defense is positioned.

◆ ◆

TAKING YOUR LEAD

For young players we recommend a basic, two-and-a-half step lead off first base. Always keep your eyes on the pitcher while taking your lead. Never cross over your feet while taking a lead, or your feet may get tangled up. To increase your dis-

When taking a lead, keep your eyes on the pitcher. This will allow you to get back to first base quickly.

⊘ *Don't cross your feet when you're taking a lead. This puts you in a vulnerable position on a pickoff attempt.*

tance from the pitcher (and therefore to increase the distance of a pickoff throw), take your lead off the back edge of the base, and come back to the base at that same point. Don't hesitate to dive back to the base headfirst if you have to.

THE STOLEN BASE AND THE HIT-AND-RUN

To prepare to steal a base you should take a bigger lead than normal, but not so big as to tip your hand or put yourself in jeopardy of getting picked off. Use the crossover step to get going when you make your break as soon as the pitcher makes his first move toward home plate, and stay low in your first couple of steps.

In a hit-and-run play the runner breaks similarly to the way he would on a stolen base attempt. A good jump is not critical, but even if the jump isn't good, his first couple of steps still must be convincing of a stolen base attempt. This will force the middle infielder to cover second base. In order for the hit-and-run to be successful, you want to get that middle infielder to cover the bag. The runner in a hit-and-run situation should never get picked off.

GETTING UP WITH THE PITCH

When we talk about a baserunner getting up with the pitch, we simply mean that he's creating momentum toward the next base. This helps in getting a good jump when the ball is hit, which is often critical in terms of beating a play at the next base or taking the extra base.

We tell runners to take three shuffles toward the next base as the pitch is delivered. The timing of the last shuffle should coincide with the ball entering the strike zone. Anticipate the ball in the dirt and be ready to make your break if the ball gets far enough away from the catcher. An extra step or a split second of indecision can make all the difference on such a play.

BILL'S BALL GAME

When in doubt, slide. This applies to every base that you're approaching, with the possible exception of first base. Too many injuries can occur by indecision as you come into the base. It's also pretty embarrassing to be tagged out when you would've been safe if you had simply slid.

ON FIRST BASE

A runner on first base should pick up the third-base coach and look for signs from him. It's important to keep track of the number of outs and other runners on base. Check the defensive positioning. Look at the outfielders as well as the infielders. Take notice of the arm strength of the outfielders. All of these factors will come into play as you make the snap decision to try for an extra base, a decision you make with the benefit of anticipation.

On a fly ball with fewer than two outs—assuming you're not tagging up—go down the baseline as far as you can and still get back safely once the ball is caught. You'll often hear people say to go halfway, but that's just a general guideline. The reason you go halfway or more is so that if the ball drops in you can maximize the number of bases you can advance. On a base hit, remember to pick up the third-base coach early when going from first to third. He's your eyes as far as knowing where the ball is and deciding whether to try to score.

On an extremely long ball that you know is going to be caught, you can tag up, by waiting on the bag until the ball is caught, and then break for second. On a long fly ball that might or might not be caught, it's better to go all the way to second base and watch the play. If the ball is caught, you still have time to get back to first base; if it drops, you have put yourself in the best position to score.

Don't let the second baseman tag you on a slow-hit ground ball to second. This is because you want to force an extra throw and give the batter as much time as possible to beat the play at first base. Also keep in mind that the runner on first has a responsibility for breaking up the double play, which means hustling into second base on a ground ball and making a good, hard slide.

Always tag up on foul balls. This rule applies for all base-runners. The only way you can possibly advance on a ball hit in foul territory is by tagging up. Also, be ready to take the extra base if the fielder should fall into the stands, slip and fall—or any number of other odd things that could happen.

ON SECOND BASE

Since there's no one holding you on, you can take a little bit bigger lead off second base than you can off first. If you're not stealing, take your lead a little bit set back from the baseline. This will give you the angle you'll need to round third base when attempting to score on a hit.

While standing on the base, check out the defensive positioning. Look and see how close the second baseman and shortstop are to second base. Are the outfielders deep or shallow? Are they playing straight up or are they shifted? These will be factors in your decision of whether to try to score on a short single to the outfield.

After you've taken your lead, avoid turning around to look at the middle infielders. Keep your eyes on the pitcher. After all, he's the one with the ball. You can see the second base-man out of the corner of your eye, and you should rely on the third-base coach to give you the position of the shortstop. Stay alert for pickoff plays.

If there's no runner on first base, you must make sure that a ground ball in front of you goes through the infield before you try for third. The general rule is that on a ball hit at you or behind you (to your left), you should advance to third, but on a ball hit in front of you (to your right), make it go through to the outfield before advancing.

On a long fly ball, if you're unsure if the ball will be caught, apply this general rule: If there are no outs, you should be in a position to tag up and advance to third. If there's one out, you should be more inclined to be about halfway between second and third. The reason is pretty simple: With no outs, if the ball drops in or hits off the wall, the worst that'll happen is you'll advance to third and there still won't be any outs; the chance for a big inning is still alive. With one out, you want to be able to score the run if the ball falls in. If you were tagging and the catch was made you could advance to third, but the gain would not be that significant. If there are two outs and a man on third or two outs and a man on second, the runner is in scoring position either way, and it'll more than likely take a hit to score him.

There is another tough situation that could come up when a runner is on second base: With fewer than two outs a line drive is hit into one of the gaps. The outfielder has a chance of making a diving catch or a great running catch. The runner on second must make a good read of the play to make the right decision. After getting up with the pitch, once the line drive is hit toward the gap, the first thing the runner on second must do is freeze and take a couple of steps back toward the bag, while watching the play. You should be approximately three steps from the bag while judging the play. If the outfielder makes a spectacular play, from this position you'll have time to take the few steps back to the bag, tag up, and advance to third. If the outfielder doesn't catch the ball, you'll still score easily. And that, as we explained earlier, is more critical with one out than it is with no outs. The key in this situation is to relax and watch the play.

When approaching third base, always run hard until the third-base coach stops you. Never assume that you will not try to score. If you're held up at third, immediately find the ball. Your reaction will be much quicker if you see it with your own eyes, rather than relying on the third-base coach's direction. This is a good general rule for all baserunners: Find the ball whenever possible.

As you would on first base, always tag up on foul balls. The only way you can possibly advance on a ball hit in foul territory is by tagging up. And as mentioned earlier, be ready to take the extra base if the fielder should slip and fall.

ON THIRD BASE

We call third base the walking base. Instead of getting up with the pitch by shuffling, your movement is that of a timed walk. Start with your right foot, and as the pitcher goes into his motion, step right, left, right. The right foot should be coming down as the ball is entering the hitting zone.

Do not end up facing directly toward home plate. Your position as the pitch is delivered should still be facing the pitcher, with your head turned slightly toward home. This position allows you to go in either direction, toward home if the ball gets away or back to third.

Always take your lead in foul territory and come back to the base in fair territory. If you get hit with a batted ball in fair territory, you are out. By going back to the base in fair territory you'll be better able to get in the way of (and thus discourage) a pickoff throw from the catcher. If a thrown ball hits you, you're not out—and you may be able to score if the ball gets away.

❖ ❖ ❖ ❖ ❖ ❖ ❖ ❖ ❖ ❖ ❖ ❖ ❖ ❖ ❖ ❖ ❖ ❖ ❖ ❖

CAL'S CORNER

Run all the way through home plate. Don't let up just because there's not a play at the plate and you'll score easily. There are other baserunners trying to do their jobs and advance, and if they get thrown out for the third out before you cross the plate, the run doesn't count. Your team has worked too hard trying to score a run to have it taken away because you were loafing or celebrating too soon.

❖ ❖ ❖ ❖ ❖ ❖ ❖ ❖ ❖ ❖ ❖ ❖ ❖ ❖ ❖ ❖ ❖ ❖ ❖ ❖

BILL'S BALL GAME

When sliding at home plate, make sure you slide *through* the plate, not just *to* it. This simply means that you should start your slide later. This protects you if the catcher decides to block the plate. Never assume that you have a nice, easy path to the plate. Slide hard and slide late.

THE CONTACT PLAY

The contact play is an effective way to score a run. It's aggressive and puts pressure on the defense. The play usually is run when there's one out, a runner on third, and the infield defense is in, trying to cut off the run at the plate. The runner on third takes a slightly bigger lead than normal. He still gets off third base in the walking method (right, left, right, as described earlier). On this play the runner has to really anticipate the batter making contact with the ball. The runner needs the best possible jump to home plate, so on every pitch he has to be anticipating contact—so much so that if the pitch is swung on and missed, the runner has to really scramble to get back to third base.

The runner is not trying to read whether it's a fly ball or a ground ball or a line drive. He's simply breaking when the bat makes contact with the ball. If there's a line drive at one of the infielders, not only will that runner be doubled off, he *should* be doubled off. If it's a line drive or a fly ball to the outfield, the runner can change his direction from going toward home plate to going back to third and tagging up. A fast runner is not required for this play. Anticipation and an aggressive jump are what's needed.

During the contact play—and this is very important—if you know you're dead at the plate, you must stop and get into a rundown to give the hitter time to get to second base, thus keeping a man in scoring position. If you have a chance of making it home, then go for it all the way.

Here's a good method in a rundown for getting the hitter to second base: Get in a position where the defense is running you toward home plate. You can accomplish this by making the defense throw the ball to home on the initial play. As soon as the infielder delivers the ball to home, stop in the baseline and create space between yourself and the catcher with the ball. Now make a quick, sudden move as if you're trying to get back to third, to force the catcher to throw the ball there. The ball is now in the third baseman's hand, and you should make him run you all the way to home. This should allow enough time to get the hitter to second. And not only have you eaten up time, you've also made the throw to second more difficult. Just by forcing the rundown toward home plate you've made the defense have to throw the ball 127 feet to try to stop the hitter from advancing into scoring position. If the rundown goes toward third base and the tag is made close to third, the throw to second will be only 90 feet—a big difference.

Let's examine what could happen from the offensive side on the contact play. If the ball is not hit directly at an infielder, you have a very good chance of scoring. The defense has to come up with a good play to throw you out. You've put pressure on the defense. If the ball is hit directly at an infielder, you read the play and decide that you're a dead out at home, so you get into a rundown and allow the hitter to get to second base. With two outs your team still has a man in scoring position. It was worth the risk: If you had played it safe and not put on the contact play, a grounder to the infield would've resulted in an out, and you would've been left with essentially the same situation: two outs and a man in scoring position.

◆ ◆

PERFECT PRACTICE MAKES PERFECT: BASERUNNING DRILLS

Relays are one way to work on baserunning skills in practice. Another useful exercise is to create track lanes, or road lanes, to demonstrate how to make proper turns. Coaches can also use stopwatches to turn the competition inward.

◆ ◆

◆ ◆

FUN FACTOR: SLIP AND SLIDE

A wet, rain-covered field doesn't necessarily mean that practice has to be a total washout. It can be a fun and enjoyable setting for sliding practice. Even on dry, hot days the use of a slip-and-slide mat can make sliding practice fun.

◆ ◆

THE BASERUNNER'S CHECKLIST

- When you're on deck, it's your job to help the runner coming to the plate.
- You don't have to be fast to be a good baserunner.
- When you hit a ground ball, don't watch the ball. Take a straight line to first and run through the bag. Hit the bag with either foot and aim for the front of the bag.
- Don't slide into first base. It slows you down and exposes you to unnecessary injury.
- On a base hit, gradually create a line as you approach each base so that you can round the bag. Don't make a keyhole or question mark turn at first base.
- Use each base to push off toward the next base.
- Always know where the ball is.
- Think in terms of two bases at a time until a fielder stops you.

- When in doubt, slide (with the possible exception of first base).
- Know the situation and anticipate the action. Always check the defense and know how many outs there are.
- Your normal lead should be about two or two and a half steps. Don't cross your feet when taking a lead. Get up with the pitch, and use the crossover step.
- Your lead off second base should be a bit bigger, and generally back in the baseline.
- Off third base take a walking lead (right, left, right) in foul territory and come back in fair.
- Don't rely on the base coaches as a crutch.
- Tag up on all foul balls.
- Run all the way through home plate.
- Slide *through* home plate, not just *to* it.

ON THE MOUND

Keys to Successful Pitching

FIRST THINGS FIRST

By Bill Ripken

Elsewhere in this book, Cal talks about how defense wins championships. I agree. Very rarely will you see a team that just sends nine guys to the plate who can really swing the bat—but can't catch and throw—win consistently over a long season. However, I'd like to take that thought one step further: Defense *and* pitching win championships. And to go even deeper, pitching is the first line of defense. The old adage that good pitching beats good hitting is true. A good pitcher on the top of his game can dominate a good-hitting club. Pitching is the single most important part of baseball. After all, the game can't start until the first pitch is thrown.

At the youth level, pitchers can set the tempo in a different way. A young pitcher who can throw strikes consistently allows the game to be played the way it should be played from a developmental standpoint. More balls are put in play by the batters when a pitcher throws strikes, which in turn allows the fielders more opportunities to make plays and experience the various game situations that will help them grow as players.

There's more to teaching pitching than most coaches realize. Have you ever been to a game and heard the following shouted from the dugouts or the bleachers?

Throw strikes!
Bend your back!
Make an adjustment!

These are some of the things I've heard at every level of baseball. I'd like to address them one by one:

Throw strikes: Don't you think the pitcher is trying to throw strikes? I'm sure if he could he would.

Bend your back: I'm assuming that they're talking about the follow-through. But I have to think that most young pitchers don't understand when or where they're supposed to bend their backs. This can create a variety of mechanical breakdowns.

Make an adjustment: This one is my all-time favorite. You even hear this at the big league level. Which adjustment?

The key thing when it comes to pitching is that there has to be a connection between the advice coming out of the dugout and the pitcher on the mound. Simply shouting general instructions isn't going to help if the pitcher and coach aren't on the same page.

That's why John Habyan, who coordinates our pitching instruction, is so valuable as a teacher. John has a way of breaking down a pitcher's mechanics, which he calls the Five Links of the Chain, that allows a coach to easily determine what part of the delivery a pitcher needs to correct and to communicate that to the player effectively.

John Habyan is not a household name. He didn't throw 95 miles per hour and didn't have dominant natural ability. What he did was figure out how to get big league hitters out consistently enough to build up eight years of major league service time and to pitch for parts of 11 seasons in the big leagues. His career numbers include an ERA below 4.00 while pitching in a middle relief and setup role.

John, or Habes as we like to call him, was drafted the same year I was, 1982, and we spent a lot of time together as teammates, roommates, and friends while we progressed through the Baltimore Orioles' minor league system. He played with Cal and me at the big league level and also played for Dad. As Cal said up front, one of the things that was important to us when we first started talking about impacting youth baseball and assembling our core staff of instructors was to bring in guys who had a connection to us and to Dad. Habes has that connection. In fact, there were times when he was struggling a little bit and searching for answers that Habes would search out Dad, whether it was on a bus trip or a plane ride, to see if Dad could help him find the answers.

Because of my relationship with Habes and the time he spent with Dad, Cal and I were confident that he would break pitching down and teach it in a way that would make us comfortable. He has done that and more for years. I think the one thing that people are most pleasantly surprised about when they attend one of our camps or clinics is the quality of pitching instruction that we provide. Most of that can be attributed to Habes.

As you will see later in this chapter, our Five Links of the Chain make it very simple for a coach to break down a pitcher's mechanics and figure out specifically what needs to be corrected. A coach may be shouting something out of the dugout that doesn't really help the pitcher. The general advice that many coaches give isn't going to allow a young pitcher to make the connection necessary to make the proper adjustment. A coach may be saying, "Bend your back," and focusing on the end of the delivery, when something very early in the delivery, something as simple as the pitcher's feet or grip, is what really needs to be corrected.

In addition to Habes's extensive knowledge of pitching, Cal and I had the good fortune as high school pitchers to have Cal Sr. as our personal pitching coach. We grew up around the game and grew up around Dad, so his insight allowed us to make the necessary connection with the various parts of our deliveries that needed improvement at a given time.

Cal even breaks down our Five Links into more simple terms to help coaches of really young players. It's not enough to tell a pitcher, especially a young one, to throw strikes. A connection has to be made with a young pitcher so that the light bulb turns on and the player understands what needs to be corrected. If a young pitcher knows what's wrong with his delivery, he can usually make the correction. The simplicity with which we approach pitching mechanics allows for young pitchers to make that connection and develop their deliveries properly. That information will be shared with you in this chapter. Enjoy it and use it to your advantage!

START BY WATCHING

As a pitching coach the majority of your time is spent behind the mound observing the pitcher, at various angles, as he throws. During this stage, especially when studying a pitcher for the very first time—and even before you've even seen him throw his first pitch—it's important that we resist the temptation to discuss any theories or expectations. Simply give him the ball and let him throw for about five to ten minutes, saying little or nothing. It's during this observation period that the good pitching instructor will look for three basic skills:

1) Is the pitcher throwing strikes?
2) Does the pitcher have good velocity?
3) Does the pitcher have good movement on his ball?

Why these three and not mechanics? The answer is simple. The more a pitcher executes these three essential skills, the less you have to do as a coach. The pitcher is doing a lot of things right if these three things are happening.

Furthermore, by focusing on the results of his pitches first, rather than his mechanics, you protect yourself from tinkering with pitchers who throw well but have unconventional mechanics. This isn't to say that smooth and fluid mechanics aren't a crucial requirement when throwing a baseball. Nevertheless, if you come across a pitcher who's herky-jerky, but is throwing strikes, having success, and experiencing no pain as a result of his motion, do you break him down and change him? We would say no.

In the major leagues you'll see pitchers with picture-perfect mechanics and others with not-so-perfect mechanics. Every pitcher's mechanics are going to be a little different. The one important similarity for pitchers who throw strikes, despite the differences in their mechanics, is that they get to their release point on time. We stress the importance of celebrating each player's individual style and talent. This fundamental truth is second to none when teaching the art of pitching. Just turn on the TV and you'll see that no two pitchers are exactly the same.

THROWING STRIKES

We often ask our young pitchers this question: What's the best pitch in baseball? The responses we get usually vary from the four-seam fastball to the slider, or even the split-fingered fastball. We then explain that all those choices are very good pitches, but are ineffective if they aren't thrown for strikes. We then stress that strike one is without a doubt the best pitch in baseball.

As a pitching coach it's extremely important that we make throwing strikes a major priority in the development of the young pitcher. It's the first skill we try to teach. Velocity is relative based on the age group, but can be improved by throwing fastballs a majority of the time. Ball movement is a more advanced concept that comes into play as a pitcher matures.

So how do we get a young pitcher to throw strikes? Do we start tinkering with his mechanics yet? Not so fast.

GRIPS

The first thing we look at with a pitcher is to make sure that he's holding the ball properly. The first two grips we introduce are the four-seam and two-seam fastball. We explain the difference between the two and the movement that you're supposed to get out of each pitch.

We continue to reinforce that arm strength and velocity will improve by throwing a majority of fastballs. The fastball is your foundation.

FOUR-SEAM FASTBALL

The first thing to introduce, especially to a young pitcher, is the four-seam fastball. Ask to see how the pitcher is holding the ball when he throws the four-seamer. He should be holding the ball *across* the four seams. There are two ways to do this. When you look at a basebll, you'll see that the seams form what looks like a horseshoe. You have the open end of the horseshoe and the closed end of the horseshoe. The best way is the one that the pitcher is throwing strikes with. But for a pitcher with smaller hands it's a little better fit with the open end of the horseshoe closest to the index finger. Since the index finger is shorter, with the index finger closer to the open end of the horseshoe, the seam drops down and allows the pitcher to make contact with the seam with both fingertips. For the older pitcher with bigger hands it doesn't matter as much, but for the young guys that's a good first step.

The next thing to look at is how wide the fingers are apart. You can't have the fingers too far apart, because the wider they are, the more velocity the pitcher is going to lose. The fingers should be a comfortable distance apart for that individual. A common mistake is for the thumb to creep up the side of the ball. It's really hard to throw strikes if the thumb isn't below the ball, serving as the anchor. It doesn't have to be all the way under, just more underneath the ball than on the side. Everybody has heard the expression "Hold it like an egg." This really holds true. You want a nice, easy grip. The ball should come out like a feather. The fingertips are on the

With the four-seam grip the fingertips should have contact with the seams and the thumb should be under the ball.

⊘ *This is an incorrect four-seam grip. Notice that the fingertips aren't touching the seams.*

⊘ *This is another incorrect four-seam grip. The thumb is riding up on the ball, instead of being under the ball.*

seams to generate the proper rotation, which helps movement and velocity. We want to make sure there's contact with the seams. You don't want to ride too high so the fingertips are not touching the seams.

What's the four-seam fastball going to do for you? It's going to stay straight. It's a good foundation for throwing strikes. As the pitcher evolves and gets a little bigger and stronger, there might be a little action, or movement, on the end of the four-seamer. But with the younger kids a four-seam fastball is going to stay pretty much straight—and that's good. That's why infielders and outfielders use the four-seamer on their throws, and why the four-seamer is the foundation for a pitcher to throw strikes.

TWO-SEAM FASTBALL

Once you've talked about the four-seam fastball, which is straight velocity, you can discuss trying to generate some movement. That's where the two-seam fastball comes into play. The pitcher should hold the two-seamer *with* the seams. As with the four-seamer, make sure the fingers are a comfortable distance apart and that the pitcher is not riding up on the ball. When riding up on the ball with a two-seam fastball, the fingers are splitting further apart because the seams are further apart, and the pitcher is losing velocity. The fingers should be working with the top half of the ball where the

On the two-seamer the fingers should also be in contact with the seams.

⊘ This is an incorrect two-seam grip. The fingers are riding too far up the seams.

seams are the closest together. Whether the pitcher grips the ball with the fingers on top or inside the seams depends on comfort level. The key is to figure out which grip allows the pitcher to throw strikes while achieving maximum velocity and movement. Once again, make sure the thumb is below the ball.

If you're a righthander throwing to a righthanded hitter, the two-seamer is supposed to run inside. If you're a left-handed pitcher, it's just the opposite: It should move away from a righthanded hitter. How is that accomplished? Just like with the four-seamer, by staying behind the ball. Sometimes you'll see a two-seamer that is cutting dramatically. Many times that happens when the pitcher is coming around the ball. It's not a real natural movement, so that's not a good thing. We want to create movement by staying behind the ball and letting it come out of the hand naturally. That allows the movement to take over.

Again, keep in mind with the different ways to grip the fastball that we want to throw strikes, and the grip that allows the individual pitcher to more easily throw strikes takes precedence over movement of the ball.

MECHANICS: THE FIVE LINKS OF THE CHAIN

When the pitcher has the base—the two fastball grips—then the coach can start talking about mechanics. As a coach, sometimes you're looking at the pitcher and all you see are arms and legs coming at you. It can be tough to decipher exactly what's going on. What the coach has to do is break it down. It's really tough to look at a pitcher in his entirety while he's throwing and determine what the problem is. You may have a pitcher who has good velocity and isn't throwing strikes, but you can't tell what's wrong when looking at the entire throwing motion. You have to look at it piece by piece.

Pitching mechanics can be broken down into five sections. We call them the Five Links of the Chain. Mechanics is one continuous motion, but there are five links to that motion, and if one of those links breaks down, it can affect the chain. So as a coach it's best to look at the overall windup and then make it easier on yourself by breaking it down into the following five parts:

1) Footwork

The first thing to look at is the pitcher's feet. See where the pitcher is on the mound. There are a lot of theories. Some people say lefthanders should be on the left side of the mound and that righthanders should be on the right side of the mound. Our theory is that the pitcher should stand wherever he produces strikes. That's the comfortable spot. Are there advantages to standing on one side or the other? Sure,

The starting position is all about footwork. It's a good idea to start with your heels on the rubber and your toes in contact with the ground.

when you get to the higher levels. But at the beginning the key is to make sure the pitcher is comfortable and throwing strikes. The middle of the mound is a good starting point.

Next, we want to make sure that the pitcher is standing with his heels on the rubber and his toes touching the ground in front of the rubber. By placing his feet this way, he puts himself in a better position to execute the next move, which is the pivot. In contrast, if the pitcher starts with his feet on top of the rubber and steps back, to complete the pivot he has to pick up his foot and find the ground again. Many of the fields that kids play on have rubbers that after a couple of days have four-inch gullies in front of them. So if you get a young pitcher picking up his foot and finding the spot and then dropping four inches again, it's going to be tough for him to throw strikes. Many times we overanalyze the mechanics of pitchers who are struggling to throw strikes when the problem could just be a simple thing like the feet or the pitching mound.

You should then look at what type of tempo the pitcher has. Is the first step nice and smooth, or is it violent? We have to make sure the pitcher has a nice, smooth first step. A good indicator when a pitcher takes the first step back is to look at the head and the pivot foot. Does the head remain over the pivot foot? If the pitcher strays too far back, the head is going to go with the foot. So an easy thing to tell a pitcher instead of worrying about the feet is to say, "Keep your head above your pivot foot." That automatically will make the pitcher take a shorter step back and slow the tempo down.

Also, make it clear that saying "Take a step back" doesn't literally mean "Take a step straight back." Actually, the majority of pitchers take a step back at a 45-degree angle. Some take a step to the side. The important thing is that it feels comfortable. The next thing to look at is the pivot. Make sure young pitchers pivot all the way so that their foot is totally parallel to the rubber. If they don't, if they get lazy and spin their heel on top of the rubber or leave the foot at a 45-degree angle to the rubber, when they get to balance position they're already pointing away from home plate. They're too open and are self-destructing before they start. That's the first link—it's all feet.

Left: *A small first step back allows the head to stay over the pivot foot.*

Right:
⊘ *A big first step back can create problems early in the windup.*

Left: *Make sure your pivot foot makes a full pivot parallel with the rubber.*

Right:
⊘ *If the pivot foot doesn't make a full pivot, you could self-destruct before you even start.*

CAL'S CORNER

Before he starts his motion, the pitcher should have the ball in his glove so the hitter can't see it and doesn't know what's coming. You don't only want to hide the ball, you want to hide your hand so the hitter can't see your grip. If you hold the ball behind you, the opposing base coach can get an idea as to your grip and what pitch you're throwing. So use your glove to shield the pitch from the hitter and the base coach. Also bear in mind that when the pitcher starts his footwork, some will keep the glove still, like Mike Mussina of the New York Yankees, and some will prefer to bring the glove over their head, like Mussina's former teammate David Wells. There's no right or wrong way as long as the pitcher feels comfortable with his tempo and timing. Remember that a pitcher who prefers to bring the glove over his head needs to do that at the same time as he makes his first step back. After that the pivot takes place and the glove and the knee will meet in the balance position.

2) Balance Position

Next you want to see how the pitcher brings his front leg up into what we call the balance position. Is it a controlled movement or is it violent? The pitcher should be in control of that leg. In the balance position, the angle of the leg should be slightly closed. If the pitcher's leg is not slightly closed, with the butt cheek pointing toward the catcher, he's opening up too soon, thus causing him to land awkwardly and taking his direction away from the catcher.

As the front leg comes up, look at how the pitcher brings his hands and legs together. This is where the pitcher gathers. It should be comfortable and there should be a slight pause, though not a long one. The pitcher gathers at balance position and

Bring your upper and lower body together to form the balance position. When a pitcher picks up his front leg, the hands need to gather with the front knee.

⊘ When bringing your front leg up, don't lean too far back.

then goes toward the plate. If you're talking textbook-perfect mechanics, then the glove should be slightly above the knee. However, you may come across pitchers who have a high leg kick and keep their glove low or have a low leg kick and keep their glove high. Remember that the key words here are *balance* and *gather*. If the pitcher is doing those two things correctly, he'll put himself in a better position to throw strikes.

As a pitcher you have to use your legs. Your legs are always going to be stronger than your arm. You might say, "I've got a strong arm, I don't need to use my legs that much." That may be true, but if so, you're only going to be a two- or three- or four-inning pitcher, because you're going to get tired more quickly than a pitcher who uses his legs. A pitcher who has a strong arm and uses his legs is one who's going to get to the 6th, 7th, or 8th inning.

3) Power Position

Getting a young pitcher into the correct power position is a crucial element in the quest to enhance velocity, create movement, and, most important, throw strikes. There are many things to look at when a pitcher gets to this link, so it's more

Below: *When going from the balance position to the power position, the pitcher must take the baseball down, out, and up from his glove with his hand on top of the ball.*

important than ever that we break things down and take them one step at a time.

When a pitcher is coming out of his balance point, the power position is formed *(page 75, photo on right)* when the pitcher does these three things:

1) Removes the ball from the glove.
2) Gets the front shoulder and arm on the target.
3) Strides toward the plate.

The first thing we want to focus on is how the pitcher is taking the ball out of the glove. Initially the hand and the ball will come out of the glove on a downward angle and then move upward, starting what will eventually be a circular movement. The key here is to make sure that the hand and fingers are on top of the ball. This will allow the pitcher to create arm action. Arm action is created when the hand goes from above the ball to behind the ball when a pitcher is throwing *(page 77, both photos)*. What the pitcher wants to avoid is getting his hand underneath the ball. If this occurs, he will be unable to create correct arm action and form the proper L. This problem is easy to spot, because the pitcher's arm action looks similar to that of a pitching machine: It's very straight with little torque.

Next we want to make sure that the front shoulder and arm are pointing toward the target. At this stage the front arm is critical, as it provides direction toward the strike zone. If the front arm is not used, it's like sailing a boat without a rudder: Not only will the pitcher be inconsistent throwing strikes, but he also won't be in a position to create the torque required when he gets to Link 4, which is rotation. This is not just for pitchers, but for every position. This is how you throw a baseball!

Third, when making the stride toward the plate, we want to make sure that the pitcher doesn't overstride by throwing his weight forward before he's ready. An aggressive weight shift occurs at the end of rotation and the follow-through. At this point it's important to bear in mind that the pitcher is still loading up in order to create power and momentum. During a ball game we've all heard coaches yell, "Stay back!" or "You're rushing!" Well, this is what they're talking about.

Arm action is created when the hand goes from above the ball to behind the ball while the pitcher is throwing.

4) Rotation

Up to this point we've talked about the pitcher keeping his weight back and putting himself in a position to create torque and momentum. Now is the time when he starts coming forward.

Focusing on the throwing arm, it's at this point that the hand goes from above the ball to behind the ball. As the arm comes forward, the pitcher should keep the elbow slightly above the shoulder in order to create an L with the throwing arm. Each pitcher's L will vary depending on the position of the arm slot. Meaning: Does he throw at three-quarters, straight over the top, or somewhere in between? Regardless, the elbow should remain slightly above the shoulder; it's the hand, or arm slot, that may vary from pitcher to pitcher.

Next, as the throwing arm is rotating forward, the pitcher wants to make sure his front arm is retracting. It's in this action, with the two arms working in coordination, that he generates much of the torque and momentum not only to throw hard but to maintain a level of consistency for throwing strikes.

Moving to the lower body, check to see that the hips are also rotating in sync with the upper body and that the front foot is pointing toward the target *(page 79, photo on left)*. If the front foot does not rotate, it will block off the front hip, and it may also take the pitcher's direction away from the plate. When this occurs, the pitcher is forced to compensate, and

During rotation it's important to keep the elbow above the shoulder, creating an L.

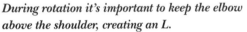 *When the elbow drops below the shoulder, the pitcher has a tendency to lose velocity and throw the ball high.*

the result is what is commonly referred to as "throwing across your body."

Before we leave rotation, we also want to take an overall look at the body and make sure that the pitcher is maintaining good posture. Even though he's rotating forward, he wants to stay tall so he can work downhill toward the plate. As shown in the photo above *(left)*, this is achieved by keeping the back foot on the rubber. A common mistake made by young pitchers is bringing the back foot forward at the same time as the throwing arm. As you can see on page 79 *(left)*, the ball is out of the hand a split second before the back foot is released.

5) Follow-Through

As we mentioned earlier, if you break a pitcher's motion down on film you should see the back foot stay back and on the ground until the ball is released. Then the follow-through takes place. The follow-through is a result of the momentum the pitcher has created through the four previous links. If the pitcher doesn't create momentum, he's not going to have a strong finish. Often, if a pitcher has a poor follow-through, he's told to bend his back. However, one should first ask, "Why isn't he bending his back?" The point is that the problem may lie in Link 3 or Link 4. In pitching, many times the problem isn't at the spot where you're seeing it—it's before.

Not everybody is going to have the same form of momentum. Not every pitcher is going to be able to generate momentum and follow through to a perfect fielding position. Does it help? Sure. Is it a necessity? No. Years ago, Goose Gossage used to end up practically down the first-base line. He had a Hall of Fame career. Can you imagine if his youth league coach had tried to straighten him out at twelve years old? The point is that he was able to throw strikes despite that finish. That's because he was on time with his release point when he needed to be. He just had so much explosiveness that his momentum carried him toward first base. A current example of this is Troy Percival of the Anaheim Angels.

When the pitcher releases the ball, both feet are on the ground.

If the four prior links are done correctly, your follow-through will take care of itself.

The Five Links are the basis. A coach should look at a pitcher and evaluate what he does. First look at the four-seam fastball and the two-seam fastball, and see if the end result is strikes. Then break down the mechanics. Block out all the rest and look at each individual link. Look at the feet, then the balance position, and after that the power position, and so on. That makes locating problems much easier. The challenge is to teach the kids the Five Links so that they know what you're talking about when you yell instructions from the dugout.

But a coach can't offer assistance unless he first watches what the pitcher is doing. If the player is having success, even though everything mechanically is not necessarily by the book, you might continue to watch, but you don't want to fix something that isn't broken. The observation and evaluation period is crucial. And before you can do anything as a coach, you have to know what you're looking at with regard to talent, whether the pitcher is or isn't having success, and where and how to give your opinion.

◆ ◆

CAL'S CORNER

The Five Links of the Chain is an advanced concept geared more toward high school pitchers. For younger players, the concept can be broken down into simpler terms:

1) Start with a baby step back.
2) Turn your foot (pivot).
3) Pick up your front leg.
4) Point your front shoulder.
5) Release the ball.

◆ ◆

WARMING UP

Teaching a young pitcher how to prepare before a game or practice is a crucial element in his overall development. Developing a routine will not only lead to more consistency on the mound, but will also help reduce the risk of injury.

Stretching followed by wind sprints should be a part of any pitcher's pre-mound ritual. These not only aid flexibility but also get the pitcher's body temperature up and blood flowing. Also, playing some light long-toss will help develop arm strength and reinforce the concept of getting full extension on the fastball. Now that we're loose, let's get on the mound.

The necessary warm-up time for most young pitchers is twelve to fifteen minutes. Start off slowly, with gradual increases in velocity. Your practice or pre-game session should start with establishing your fastball on both sides of the plate. Get in the habit of moving your catcher inside and outside. When you've established your fastball, move to your off-speed pitches.

When trying to get a feel for a particular pitch, it can be helpful to throw your pitches in patterns. For example: five four-seamers, followed by five two-seamers, then five change-ups, and so forth. As you finish, we also recommend simulating an at-bat or two while mixing up your pitches.

EYES ON THE TARGET

It's a very basic point, but amid all the complexities of mechanics, Dad always used to say, "Keep your eyes on the target. Put your front shoulder in the glove, ball behind it." That's a simple and safe thing to tell a young pitcher. Just like when you're throwing in the outfield or infield, the pitcher should pick out a certain spot. If the pitcher is locked in and never takes his eyes off the target, that's a good starting point. If a young pitcher is taking his eyes off the target for a split second and still throwing strikes, we don't want to mess with that. But the longer a young pitcher sees the catcher's glove, the more likely it is that he's going to throw a strike.

BILL'S BALL GAME

When you watch a big league pitcher like Mike Mussina throw, look at his head and notice how his eyes are locked in on the target the whole time through his motion. There are some pitchers out there who can take their eyes off the target and get it back, but for young kids a good starting point is to say, "Look at the target, and keep your eyes on the target throughout."

OFF-SPEED PITCHES

When a pitcher can throw the two types of fastballs on both sides of the plate and has a good grasp of mechanics, then it's time to look at off-speed pitches. But we stress the importance of establishing the fastball first. Too many pitchers, especially those at the high school level, are in a hurry to become four-pitch pitchers. A good coach will stress the importance of establishing the fastball, since it's the foundation for all the other pitches.

The most important thing for off-speed pitches is to make sure that the ball is comfortable in the pitcher's hand. Often a young pitcher will see a teammate with a good curveball and try to imitate that grip, whether it's comfortable or not. Every pitcher's hand is different. Everyone has a different arm slot (this refers to whether he throws overhand or sidearm), velocity, and confidence, all of which are huge factors in throwing an off-speed pitch for a strike. The best grip is the one that feels the most comfortable in the pitcher's hand, so that's what the coach has to find.

As a pitcher you're constantly tweaking, trying to get better, especially as a youngster. You're constantly adjusting and looking for better ways to throw different pitches. As you move up the ladder you're going to have different pitching coaches. What you want to do is take the things each one says, know which points apply to you, and incorporate them into what you do.

THE CHANGE-UP

The change-up is a great pitch. If you're looking for something to teach young pitchers as an off-speed pitch, teach the change-up first. What is a change-up supposed to do? It's an off-speed pitch, which means you're trying to take something off the fastball. Depending on the velocity range, the change-up is going to be 8 to 10 miles per hour slower than the fastball. The pitcher wants to have arm speed and action similar to that of the fastball, but the pitch actually is a little bit slower. The idea is to throw off the hitter's timing and get his weight out in front too soon, eliminating his power. This can be a difficult concept for young pitchers to apply because they've been told all their lives to throw hard, and all of a sudden you're telling them to throw easier. They have to be convinced about what the change-up is designed to do—get the batter's weight out in front—and that they should trust the pitch. The change-up is thrown for a strike, but it's not a strikeout pitch. Let the batter hit it. Get that point across as well, so the pitcher has the confidence to throw it.

The assumption on the change-up grip is that the ball needs to be back in the hand. It's still thrown with the fingers.

⊘ Having the ball jammed back into the hand makes it very difficult to throw a change-up for strikes.

It may be helpful in the early stages to stress the importance of throwing it for a strike and letting the batter hit it, rather that using it as a strikeout pitch. In time it may develop into a strikeout pitch, but the emphasis should be on throwing strikes and not on how much the pitcher can make it move.

There are a variety of change-up grips. There's a three-finger grip that's good for younger pitchers with smaller hands. You grab the ball across the four seams or two seams, whichever is more comfortable. Get three fingers on it, but make sure the pitcher doesn't stick the ball in the back of his palm. One of the myths about a change-up is that you have to jam it into your palm and choke it. Not true. When you grip the ball, place it in the back of your fingers, making sure there's some space between your palm and the ball. You throw a baseball with your fingers, not your hand. Some guys can throw a palm ball, but that's a very advanced pitch. If you're working with an eight- or nine-year old, just tell him to put three fingers on the ball with his thumb on the bottom, and throw the ball the way he would his fastball.

When the kids start getting more advanced, we can get four fingers involved. Stick the ball right in the fingers with two fingers on the middle of the ball, using the pinkie and pointer as bookends. Make sure it feels good, then have the pitcher put his thumb on the ball. If the pitcher has long fingers, this may allow for his index finger and his thumb to touch. If you can achieve this, you have the makings of what's known as a circle change. If the pitcher doesn't have long fingers, you still have a change-up grip. Don't feel the need to force the circle. It'll come. If a pitcher can't grip it that way when he's ten, he'll grow into it by the time he's sixteen. The ball has to feel comfortable in the hand in order for the pitcher to be able to throw the pitch for a strike. Move the ball around and alter the grip until it feels good. This grip takes off the velocity but allows the arm speed to remain the same as it is when a fastball is thrown.

When practicing the change-up, make sure your hand is above the ball when you take it out of the glove. As you come into rotation, your arm comes into the position, and you release the ball out in front, your hand will be slightly inside the ball. The hand naturally finishes a little inside. With the change-up, let the natural hand action create the rotation. Don't try to do too much with it. If you look at the grip, most of the pressure is on the inside of the ball anyway. The grip alone is going to take care of a lot of the action, so don't try to create too much movement. A lot of times pitchers will try to turn it over, much like a screwball, and get too much movement. Then they won't be able to keep the ball in the strike zone.

Velocity is important, but don't worry if the pitch is being thrown too hard at first. That's okay—the grip can be adjusted to take off the velocity. A lot of times, though, a young pitcher babies the pitch and kind of lobs it up there, which is worse than throwing too hard.

As coaches, we're looking to build arm strength in young players. It sounds simple, but you learn to throw hard by throwing hard. You have to throw your fastball. You throw your change-up off your fastball. You're not going to throw your fastball off your change-up. Restrict what young pitchers can throw. You can't stress enough that young pitchers shouldn't fall in love with their off-speed pitches, because in the developmental stages of a young arm the fastball is the most important pitch. Make sure you aren't allowing them to throw 50 or 60 percent off-speed pitches. They may experience success at first, but if they don't develop the fastball, they're going to fall off the ladder that you climb to get to the highest level of baseball. It's good to introduce the change-up and get the concept out there. They're going to use it as they go up the ladder, but also make sure that they throw plenty of fastballs. The fastball can be four weapons: It can be thrown high, low, inside, and outside.

Look at Jamie Moyer of the Seattle Mariners. His fastball is, tops, 84/85 miles per hour. His change-up is about 71. All he throws is fastball, change-up. But he has a great change-up and he knows how to pitch. He mixes in two or three slow curveballs a game, just to make them think he might throw it. He moves the ball around, but he can throw his fastball anywhere he wants to and his change-up anywhere he wants to.

When you're dealing with your change-up or even your

breaking ball, you have to be able to throw it for a strike or it's useless. You see guys with great breaking balls, but if they can't locate it, then it doesn't matter. If they can't throw it for strikes, the hitters will say, "Oh, breaking ball, I'll take it. I'll wait for a fastball." But if you throw your off-speed pitches for strikes, you'll become less predictable. The hitter can't just sit back and wait for your fastball.

BREAKING BALLS

One common theme with all breaking balls is that the pitcher should find a long seam. The middle finger should be placed on the inside part of the long seam so there's something to pull down on. The ball should be visible on both sides of the fingers. A common mistake of young pitchers is to have too much of the ball exposed on one side. Once in a while they'll throw one for a strike, but most times the ball just pops out and hangs. No matter what type of breaking ball is being thrown, the ball should be visible on both sides of the fingers.

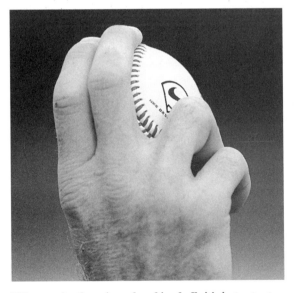

When you're throwing a breaking ball, it's important for your middle finger to be able to find and use a long seam.

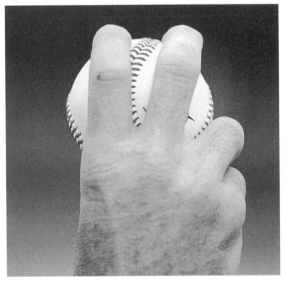

⊘ On a breaking ball, finding a long seam but not using it is not beneficial.

You still throw the breaking ball out front, but with the breaking ball (left) you don't use as much extension as with the fastball (right).

Some pitchers will have a little more space between the ball and their thumb. Some will choke it off a little bit more, or grab it a little bit tighter. You have to constantly tweak it. The coach should tell the pitcher to move the grip around and throw a few to see what's comfortable. The most important thing is for it to feel good in the pitcher's hand.

The progression of the windup is the same as with a fastball at the beginning. The hand stays on top of the ball all the way through into rotation before the hand gets over the ball out in front of the body. Young pitchers have a tendency to drop their hand under the ball to throw a breaking ball. But this type of pitch won't get much better, and it puts too much strain on the elbow. As the arm gets in front of the body, the hand should come over on top of the ball and then through it. This is where confidence comes in—getting in front and being aggressive with it.

When you throw a breaking ball, you want to have good extension, but not quite as much as a fastball after the pitch is released. To get the feel for this, have someone hold a glove out where the pitcher would normally extend to after releasing the ball. Make sure the pitcher pulls back in after rotation and follows through short of the normal follow-through.

As far as visualization, when you tell a pitcher to throw a breaking ball for the first time, make the expectation small. You've heard the term *breaking ball*. All we're trying to do is take a ball and make it break. We don't say *curveball* or *slider*. We let the pitcher determine which breaking ball he has. Just get the hand out in front and create some rotation. A lot of times you tell a player to throw a curveball and he has certain expectations because he's seen a big league pitcher throw one that breaks off the table. Then the first thing the player tries to do is make the ball break from very high to very low. Tell the catcher to ask the pitcher to make the break small. Create some rotation and throw some strikes.

You can start the pitcher out in the power position drill practicing breaking balls from a shortened distance. It's an easy way, from the shorter distance, to get the pitcher comfortable with the ball coming out of his hand. The more comfortable the pitcher gets, the further back the catcher can move.

Young pitchers often force the issue and throw the ball up to make it break down. The key is to get the hand over the ball and let the ball break a little bit. There's a fine line between overthrowing it and being firm with it. You want to be firm, but you don't want to throw wildly.

Remember: If you teach a pitcher a good breaking ball at a young age, don't let him fall in love with it. Young pitchers should be building arm strength by throwing mostly fastballs. If they fall in love with the curveball, they won't strengthen their arms sufficiently, and as they get older their velocity will suffer and the risk of injury will be greater.

You don't develop a good curveball when you're ten years old and take it to the big leagues. You develop a good curveball by throwing a lot of fastballs at a young age. That strengthens the arm so that when it's time to develop a breaking ball, the pitcher is able to do so. But first you have to establish a fastball to build up arm strength. It's a God-given gift to be able to throw hard, but if you keep throwing fastballs, you'll develop your arm strength and allow yourself to throw a better fastball. The more breaking balls a pitcher throws at a young age, the more miles per hour it's going to take off his fastball as he gets older. But if you develop a good fastball as a youngster, then you're going to be able to throw a good breaking ball when you get older.

There's nothing wrong with a coach introducing the concepts of the breaking ball, but the coach has to manage the big picture and set certain rules. If a pitcher wants to go to the big leagues, his arm strength and fastball are going to get him there. He can add a breaking ball as he goes, but he should minimize it. When a young player does start developing breaking pitches, the coach should not have him try to throw it for the sake of winning the game. The coach can't compromise his rules and principles that govern the player's development. The concept of the breaking ball is good, because if a pitcher understands it, he can grow with the concept as he gets older. The coach, however, has to make sure he minimizes the use of the pitch in games.

FIELDING

It's important for a pitcher to remember that once he releases the ball, he's no longer a pitcher, he's a fielder. So he has to get into position after delivering the pitch and field those balls hit back to him. A pitcher fields a ground ball just like any other infielder: wide base, butt down, hands out in front. To combine pitching and fielding work, coaches can mix in some comebackers in practice when pitchers are throwing off the mound.

Pitchers who get hit with a ball or knock a ball down should not panic. There's plenty of time. The runner is barely out of the box; he still has 85 feet or so to run. Just make sure you pick up the ball the first time, with your bare hand. Stay in control and slow the game down.

Besides comebackers, fielding bunts is also a useful skill to work on with pitchers in practice. Coaches should stress footwork. On bunts down the first-base line, a righthander opens up to first base, fields the ball, generates momentum toward the base, and throws. A lefthander fields the ball so that his left foot is between the ball and the foul line. Then he slowly

When covering first base, get over as quickly as possible, get your glove up and out in front of you, and be a good target for your first baseman.

turns his body glove-side to make the throw to first. Lefthanders have to be careful not to open up too far, but they still want to generate momentum and point their front shoulder toward the target for the throw. On bunts down the third-base line you reverse the footwork when throwing to third. Coaches can also work with pitchers on the underhand flip to first. With the underhand flip it's still important to generate momentum toward the target; you want to eliminate too much arm swing, or "bowling."

COVERING FIRST

When your pitchers are on the mound for fielding practice or in a game, on every ball hit to the right side of the infield—no matter if it's a foul ball, a fly ball, or whatever—their first instinct has to be to get over to first base. And it has to be an instinct. If you throw a pitch and the ball is hit to the right side and you have to wait for someone in the dugout to yell at you to get over there, it's going to be too late. That's the single biggest element of this play: The pitcher has to be quick getting over to first. If he's not, the play is going to be a lot more difficult than it should be.

So on every ball hit to the right side, pitchers should focus on taking that first step to that side. This way if it's a ground ball to the first baseman and the pitcher is in the play, he's already a step in the right direction. The pitcher's responsibility if the ground ball is hit to the first baseman is to get over to cover that bag. How do we do that? Pick out a spot fifteen to twenty feet up the first-base line. The pitcher should run to that spot hard. When you get to that spot, back off and get under control. Get your glove up and ask for the ball. You want the first baseman to know that you're ready. Catch the toss first and then keep running and touch the base with your right foot. Stay in fair territory after you touch the base. If you touch the base with your left foot or cross into foul territory you're going to be in the baseline and the baserunner is going to run up your back. The reason you get under control is that if the first baseman bobbles the ball, you have to be able to stop on the bag and become a first baseman and finish the play. It's important to run hard, get under control, and make a read on the play. You're either going to get the ball on the run or stop at the bag.

THE STRETCH POSITION: THE DELIVERY AND HOLDING RUNNERS

When there are runners on base, a pitcher must work from the stretch position as opposed to the full windup. For righthanded pitchers, this means you will start off by placing your right foot alongside the rubber, with your back toward first base. For lefthanded pitchers, it's the opposite. When you first come into contact with the rubber, your hands should be separated. A preferable stance is slightly bending your back toward home plate while putting your glove hand on your front knee and your throwing hand behind your lower back. This is the position you want to be in while receiving the sign from the catcher. At this point you also have the option of holding the ball in the glove or keeping it in your throwing hand. The latter is recommended because it allows you to throw over to first base at any time.

After receiving the sign from the catcher, a pitcher is ready to come to the set position. This is achieved by shifting the body to an upright position while bringing the throwing hand inside the glove in one continuous motion. Your weight should be slightly on your back leg, not leaning forward. Righthanders, make sure that your feet are not too close together, as this can make it more difficult to throw over to first base. Once you're in the set position you can move your head only when checking the runners; if you move your head and shoulders, it's a balk. You also must show the umpire that you have come to a complete and discernible stop. When delivering the ball to the plate, you want to be sure that you have no unnecessary movements (this is particularly true for right-handers). All this means is that you want to avoid being too slow to the plate. This can be achieved by having a slightly lower leg kick and speeding up your tempo. Remember that you want to be as quick as possible without sacrificing the effectiveness of your pitches. For lefthanders, being quick to the plate is not as important as being deceptive. The key is making sure your delivery is exactly the same to the plate as it is toward first. The height of your leg kick as you come to your balance position and the position of your hands should be identical in each instance.

Along with having an effective and efficient delivery, you also want to make sure you don't become a predictable pitcher. A pitcher who comes to the set position and goes to the plate the same way every time is an easy guy to steal on. You want to change your timing and patterns. This can be a very effective tool. Rickey Henderson, one of the best base stealers in the game, used to say that the pitchers who gave him the most trouble were the ones who held the ball on him. What that forces the runner to do is stop. If he's on first base and he's creeping and you're coming to the set position and all of a sudden you're holding the ball on him, there's a point at which he has to say, "I'm too far from the bag. I have to stop. I can't go any further." If you hold the ball on the runner, he might land on his heels, get off the balls of his feet, and go back. He might also flinch toward second, tipping his hand that he's stealing. All because you were simply holding the ball.

Another way to keep a runner off balance is not to show them your best pickoff move every time you throw over to the base. To start off, you can just give the runner a get-it-over-there move. You want to set him up a little bit. Give him a move that's good enough that if he's sleeping you might get him. The runner might think that's your best move. He might get a larger lead. If you look over and he's creeping out a bit more, then give your best move. That's part of using your head and always thinking.

RIGHTHANDED PICKOFF: FOOTWORK

When you watch a big league pitcher make his pickoff, it happens so fast that it appears that both his feet are moving at the same time. Actually, the back foot moves a split second before the front foot. This allows the pitcher to disengage the rubber. If the front foot moves first, not only will the pitcher have poor balance (the back foot, still in contact with the rubber, will only rotate), this is a balk. Also, a pitcher should make sure that as he turns toward first base his front foot rotates all the way toward his target. Otherwise, he will throw across his body, decreasing his chances of making a good throw.

The footwork is crucial to a quality pickoff move: quick feet followed by a quick, accurate throw. A common mistake is ignoring proper footwork and just throwing the ball as hard as you can. This can lead to big trouble. The intended target should be the knees or waist of the first baseman; if you throw at the bag, the throw might get tangled up with the runner sliding back.

LEFTHANDED PICKOFF: FOOTWORK

As stated earlier, the key to a successful pickoff move for a lefthander is deception. It's convincing the runner that you're going to throw home when actually you're throwing to first, and vice versa. When making the throw, once again, footwork is vital to a successful pickoff move. For the lefty whose right

On a pickoff, break from the rubber first, then set your feet and make an accurate throw.

When trying to pick off a runner at second base, you should end up straddling the rubber.

foot crosses the plane of the rubber when he gets to his balance point an important rule to bear in mind is that although he can legally deliver the ball to the plate, he cannot cross the plane of the rubber and attempt a pickoff move. If this is the case, the pitcher must learn to deliver the ball to the plate without crossing the plane of the rubber, so that his mechanics for both a pitch and a pickoff remain identical. In addition, when making a throw to first base, how far a lefty moves his right foot toward home plate will vary. Some lefties may take the right foot in a direct line to the bag; others will end up closer to the plate. The latter is more deceptive, but remember, a pitcher shouldn't sacrifice accuracy if he (particularly a young pitcher) cannot master this technique.

Just as with the righthanded throw, a lefty should give the first baseman a chance to make a play by hitting him with the throw in the knees or the waist.

PICKOFF: SECOND BASE

At second base it's the same thing. You don't want to fall into a pattern. What we see a lot in the young age groups is: come set, one look, and go to the plate. Change your looks. One time look once. Other times give it two. Sometimes don't look over there at all. Don't be predictable. As far as the footwork, when you make your quick move over to second, again you're going to move your back foot first. You're going to turn to your glove side and your back foot is going to end up slightly in front of where your front foot was. And your front foot is going to spin and end up on the other side of the rubber so that you're straddling it. Again, quick feet, quick, accurate throw. Get your head around and see your target.

Another pickoff move you can make is a spin move, or an inside move. You come set, you come up (leg up and back toward second base), step off, and throw. You don't have to come up and try to throw the ball all at once. You just have to sell it a little bit: Make it appear to the runner that you're

The inside move is a more advanced pickoff play used at the higher levels.

throwing to the plate. Chances are when you get a runner with this move, when your leg is up, he's going to be out in no-man's-land. What you want to avoid is if you do everything at once and throw to second, if he's running, he's going to get to third base. If he does a straight steal and you don't look where he is, by the time you throw the ball to second he's going to be at third. If you pick a runner off with this move, there's most likely going to be a rundown, because he's going to be caught between the bases. If you're going to use what's called the daylight play—where you throw to second if you see daylight between the runner and the bag—use the quick move, because that needs to be a snap throw.

To practice pickoff moves, coaches can set up two pitching rubbers close to each other, with a line of pitchers at each, one throwing to first base and one throwing to second.

The one-knee drill is to help with getting the hand on top of the ball after taking the ball out of the glove.

PERFECT PRACTICE MAKES PERFECT: THE ONE-KNEE DRILL

There are various drills that can assist with pitching mechanics, but we always stress the importance of the grip. You can do all of the drills in the world, but if the pitcher isn't gripping the ball correctly, he won't improve.

The one-knee drill breaks down a pitcher's arm action and works on the power position. It concentrates on taking the ball back out of the glove and keeping the hand behind the ball. The drill is excellent for short-armers and long-armers—guys who get underneath the ball. It can be done in the outfield before a game.

The drill goes like this: Pitchers drop their throwing-side knee to the ground with the opposite knee up and play catch, using only a four-seam grip, from a short distance. They don't have to throw hard. The coach can also tell the pitcher to look back and see what his arm and hand should look like before coming forward. This may allow the player to see what he's doing wrong. As always, there are no quick fixes. Drills must be done every day in practice in order to correct problems.

The tee drill is designed to help the pitcher keep his elbow above the shoulder.

PERFECT PRACTICE MAKES PERFECT: THE TEE DRILL

This drill is for the pitcher who chronically lets his elbow drop below his shoulder. A batting tee is placed on the player's throwing side, close enough so that if his elbow drops, it'll hit the tee. This allows the pitcher to get used to the proper throwing motion. The pitcher should throw from the one-knee position (throwing-side knee to the ground). Pitchers will exaggerate the elbow position to avoid hitting the tee. On a daily basis this will help create muscle memory so the pitcher automatically does it properly.

PERFECT PRACTICE MAKES PERFECT: THE POWER POSITION DRILL

This drill can be used not only for troubleshooting, but also as a warm-up before a pitcher goes into a game. The pitcher starts by creating a wide base with his feet. Using a four-seam grip, the hand is placed on the ball in the glove at chest level. The coach should make sure the pitcher shifts his weight back before going forward. The hands break, the weight goes back, the power position is assumed, the ball is released (as with the one-knee drill, the pitcher doesn't have to throw hard), and the follow-through takes place. The follow-through in this drill occurs only with the arm. Both feet stay on the ground, with the trail foot staying near the rubber. Have the pitcher rotate on the back side, creating a nice hip turn and finish. Make sure the front toe is pointing forward.

Remember that in the power position, the hand is above the baseball, and the front shoulder is used as a sight pointing directly at the target. The first time you show this drill to your pitcher, it'll be tough, because it takes a lot of balance and timing. Have the pitcher stop and pose for a picture after the arm finishes. Both feet should be on the ground. For short-armers, have them start in the finish position and then take their weight all the way back through the power position before finishing. This creates a long, whiplike motion and gives them a feeling of stretching the throwing motion out.

Another variation of the power position drill, for pitchers who throw the ball high a lot, is to have the catcher shorten up. To throw the ball downhill to the catcher, the pitcher has to concentrate on getting the elbow up and staying on top of the ball. This isn't a velocity drill. All the pitcher is thinking about is timing and balance. This drill is also good for long-striders. Pitchers with long strides will not be able to get downhill in time. Remember that both feet are on the ground when the pitcher completes this drill. The follow-through is with the arm only, just as in the regular power position drill.

The power position drill starts in a balance position, allowing you to get your weight back to your backside, getting you into the power position itself, and creating arm action and rotation.

Pitchers can also do "dry" sets, in which they're just working on the power position and rotation movements without baseballs. Five or ten sets of each motion will help create muscle memory and will allow pitchers to better make adjustments during games when coaches point out problems.

◆ ◆

THE PITCHER'S CHECKLIST

- When watching a pitcher throw for the first time, it's important to look at whether the pitcher is throwing strikes, at velocity, and at ball movement.
- The fastball is the foundation for everything a pitcher does. You can't develop off-speed pitches without the arm strength gained by throwing a lot of fastballs at a young age.
- A pitching coach should first look at a pitcher's results before he starts breaking down that pitcher's mechanics.
- The grip is important in pitching, and the best grip for a particular pitch is the one that's most comfortable for the pitcher while allowing him to throw strikes and achieve maximum velocity and movement.
- The first pitch to introduce, especially to a young pitcher, is the four-seam fastball.

- Change-of-speed pitches should be prioritized over pitches with movement of the ball.
- Pitching mechanics is one continuous motion, but there are Five Links to that motion—footwork, balance position, power position, rotation, and follow-through—and if one of those links breaks down, it can affect the chain.
- Encourage young pitchers to keep their eyes on the target. The longer a pitcher sees the catcher's mitt, the more likely it is that he's going to throw a strike.
- The most important thing for off-speed pitches is to make sure that the ball is comfortable in the pitcher's hand.
- Coaches should not let young pitchers fall in love with their off-speed pitches and throw them too often.
- Once the pitcher releases the ball, he's no longer a pitcher, he's a fielder. A pitcher fields a ground ball just like any other infielder: wide base, butt down, hands out in front.
- On a ball to the right side, a pitcher's first instinct should be to get over to first base.
- A pitcher who comes to the set position and goes to the plate the same way every time is easy to steal on. He should change his timing and pattern when throwing to the plate, and vary the type and quality of his pickoff moves.

IN THE INFIELD

It Starts with Catching and Throwing

FIRST THINGS FIRST

By Cal Ripken, Jr.

Defense in general is not given nearly enough attention in baseball. If I were to offer a guess on why that is, I'd have to say that hitting is the glamorous side of baseball and therefore it's always center stage. But if you were to look at all the winning teams at the highest levels, it's defense that wins championships. Defense is a constant; it's more in your control, so it's ultimately the key to your team's success.

Let's take a quick snapshot of Bill's and my career: Bill and I were the double-play combination for five years in Baltimore. When people think of Bill's career, they think of a defensive specialist. He was a great second baseman, and in the latter part of his career he was valued as an infielder who could play all the positions well. Bill had some good offensive years, and he could contribute in many ways with the bat, but his value as a defensive player overshadowed his offense.

When people think of me, they automatically think of an offensive shortstop, that I helped change the mind-set of how a shortstop should be viewed. I'm proud of that, but I'm equally proud of the level of defense that I brought to the position. Actually I'm more proud of the defensive side. I broke the American League assist mark with 584 in 1983; I went 95 straight games without an error that year, and made only three errors for the entire season, a record low for a full-time shortstop. I led the league in assists, double plays, and fielding percentage many times. I don't bring all this up for bragging purposes, just to emphasize the pride I took on defense.

I've often said how great it was to be on the All-Star team because of the opportunity to be with the best players in the league. I loved sitting around with the other shortstops to compare notes. Early in my career I was around guys like Robin Yount and Alan Trammell, and later with the super-shortstops Alex Rodriguez, Derek Jeter, Nomar Garciaparra, and Miguel Tejada. Early on I would act like a sponge and try to take in all the wisdom, but later on I was the one talking and the super-shortstops were the sponges. They're all great players and we know about their offense, but all they wanted to talk about was defense. We would talk about the secret of minimizing your errors, positioning, cutoffs and relays, coverage on hit-and-runs and steals, when to take chances and when to be conservative, bunt plays, pickoffs, double plays, playing in and playing back, situations, strategies, angles to the ball, and much more.

My point is that defense is very important, and Bill and I are passionate about teaching it. This area is a challenge for us to present to you because, like hitting, it has a lot of depth as you move up the ladder. This book is a template for instruction and is meant to be broad enough for all ages, so our challenge is to stay in the basic framework. For me that's a little tough. Do you remember the book *Men at Work,* by George Will? I did the section on defense and the thoughts behind it. Many people were fascinated by its depth. I thought it was great but that we had only begun to scratch the surface.

By now you can see that Bill and I really love defense. In this chapter you'll find a framework for good, sound defense and you'll also get a glimpse of the depth. Bill loves to start off our instruction on defense with the oversimplification that defense is nothing more than catching and throwing—a big game of playing catch. Even something complex like a double play, when broken down into its simplest terms, is five parts: a catch, a throw, a catch, a throw, and a catch. When you're playing in a game at the youth level, if you start throwing the ball all over the field and guys are running around the bases like it's a merry-go-round, you won't win too many games. But when you play pretty well in the field—when you catch the ball and throw it where you're supposed to—you get outs and win games.

Everybody likes to hit in baseball more than anything else. But the better we do our job out in the field, the sooner we get to hit. If we don't do our job in the field, we're out there a long time and we can wear ourselves out, and then we're too tired to hit. We work a lot with young players on catching the ball and throwing it properly, because the better you catch and throw, the better you play the game.

CHOOSING A GLOVE

Our philosophy of celebrating the individual extends to choosing a glove. The individual player should have that freedom to choose. There are certain ideas about what size glove fits a certain type of player, but we encourage coaches to keep an open mind. Every once in a while you'll have a kid whose glove looks too big, but the coach should watch him and see how he uses it. If he uses it well and it doesn't become restrictive to the movement of his hand, leave it alone. The only requirement is to select a glove that you can handle.

❖ ❖ ❖ ❖ ❖ ❖ ❖ ❖ ❖ ❖ ❖ ❖ ❖ ❖ ❖ ❖ ❖ ❖ ❖ ❖

BILL'S BALL GAME

I used a long-fingered, deep-pocketed glove. Cal used a bigger, flatter glove. The theory used to be that middle infielders had to use a very small glove so that they could get the ball out of their glove more quickly. And generally middle infielders used to be pretty small guys. Now you've got guys who are 6'2" and 6'3" playing the middle infield positions. As long as your glove is comfortable and you can transfer the ball out of it quickly on double plays, your glove is okay. Like so many things in the game of baseball, a player should do what feels comfortable to him as long as it works.

❖ ❖ ❖ ❖ ❖ ❖ ❖ ❖ ❖ ❖ ❖ ❖ ❖ ❖ ❖ ❖ ❖ ❖ ❖ ❖

THE READY POSITION

The ready position should be one of balance and comfort, square to home plate and ready to move.

The ready position is similar to the athletic positioning you would use in almost any other sport. For infielders the primary concern is going right and left. This can be accomplished by having your feet and shoulders square to home plate, your knees slightly bent, your arms relaxed, and your weight distributed evenly on the balls of your feet in a well-balanced position. To get comfortable an infielder can creep in a little bit or move from side to side as the pitcher is preparing to deliver the ball, but the ready position must be assumed as the ball enters the hitting zone. Don't be flat-footed. Be ready to move quickly and anticipate that the ball's going to be hit to you. Know what you're going to do when that happens. As middle infielders, we preferred watching the flight of the ball as it went into the hitting zone. At first base and third base it's not as easy, so you might try focusing your eyes on the hitting zone.

Before the infielders have even taken their stances, the following should have occurred on the infield:

- The type of pitch has been signaled.
- The positioning of the infielders has been adjusted.
- The number of outs has been verified and the game situation (runners on base, etc.) reviewed.
- The man covering on a steal or hit-and-run has been determined.
- The possibility of a bunt has been considered, and an attempt has been made to anticipate the opponent's strategy.

With this mental and physical readiness, the infielders are prepared to make the play. This readiness allows you to answer that age-old question: What should I do with the ball when it's hit to me?

FIELDING A ROUTINE GROUND BALL

Every infielder should go about catching a ground ball the same way. There are three things that have to happen to catch a ground ball. We're going to start by assuming that the ball is hit right at you. The first thing that has to happen has to do with your feet. If the ball's hit right at you, what do you do with your feet? You get wide. You create a wide base. This enables you to do the second thing, which is to get your back side down as low as possible. Number three is that you have to get your hands out in front. All these things allow the next step.

If you keep your feet too narrow, you don't feel comfortable trying to get your butt down. If you get into a wide base with your butt down, your weight will be forward and your hands will almost automatically go out in front. Some coaches talk about a triangle: Your glove and your two feet form that triangle. A lot of young infielders want to catch ground balls with their glove back between their legs. There's no triangle there. But if you get your wide base, your rear end down, and your hands out in front, you can see your glove and the ball at the same time. If your hands are back, you can't. That means you have to track the ball all the way into your glove that much further. You're just making it harder on yourself. Think of it this way: If you're playing catch, and you hold your glove way back behind your head, there's a good chance the ball's going to hit you in the mouth. But if you hold your glove out in front, you can see the ball coming and you can see your glove at the same time. Then you can see the ball go into the glove. It's the same principle on a ground ball: You catch the ball out in front.

Another reason to have your hands out in front is that it puts you in a better position to react to bad hops. We all know that the conditions of most youth fields are not that good. If your hands are back

When fielding a ground ball, you should have a wide base, butt down, and hands out in front.

⊘ *Don't field a ground ball like this: feet too close together, butt too high, and head down.*

between your legs and the ball takes a bad hop, you can't get to it. You're kind of locked. But if you get in your wide base, with your rear end down and your hands out in front, and that ball takes a bad hop, your hands are free to move to the ball and then you say, "Thank you very much," and you catch that ground ball. So there are two reasons we have to have our hands out in front: We need to see the ball and the glove, and we need to be able to adjust to a bad hop.

Young infielders have heard the coach say that it's easier and faster to bring your glove up than it is to push it down. And that's true. But when the coach says to put the glove down on the ground, a lot of young infielders, even if they get into a wide base, butt down, and hands out in front, have a tendency to hold the glove flat on the ground with a stiff wrist. What chance do you have of the ball going in that glove? If the glove is down but the wrist is stiff, the ball is more likely to hit the heel of the glove, because the glove isn't at the proper angle to maximize the ball's chances of landing in it cleanly. We've all had the ball hit the heel of our glove and roll up our arm. So we take our throwing hand and put it behind our glove wrist and relax that wrist—keep it loose. If you're playing catch, you don't say, "Throw me the ball," and have your glove pointing down with a stiff wrist. No, you hold your glove so that the other player can see the inside of it. It's the same thing when you're catching a ground ball: If someone were to be standing at home plate, he should be able to see the inside of your glove.

If the fingertips of your glove touch the ground, you've created a good glove angle.

⊘ If the back of your glove is on the ground, you don't have much chance to catch the ball.

When watching a big league game, look at the proper fielding position when the ball is hit like a rocket at the infielder. Note how wide he gets, how low his rear end gets, and how far his hands get out in front. The routine ball, every now and then, is one that comes up and bites the major league player, because he's used to seeing that ball hit that way and expects to make the play. That's the time when he gets a little lax and might not be in as good a fielding position as he would be if it were a rocket.

So keep in mind that when the ball is hit harder at an infielder, his concentration almost inevitably goes up. His base gets wide, his rear end gets down, his hands get out in front, and he makes the play. If you treat every ground ball as if it's the game's most important out, you'll always be in the proper position.

◆ ◆

CAL'S CORNER

We always aspire to explain the *why*. If you remember only one thing about fielding, make it this: Get your butt down when you're fielding a ground ball. The simple reason is that you need to get your head in a position to see the ball. You can't catch it if you can't see it.

◆ ◆ ◆ ◆ ◆ ◆ ◆ ◆ ◆ ◆ ◆ ◆ ◆ ◆ ◆ ◆ ◆ ◆ ◆ ◆

◆ ◆

BILL'S BALL GAME

Omar Vizquel, who's as good a defensive infielder as there is, makes a lot of plays on the run and one-handed. It's not the way you teach young kids to play, but if you watch him closely, his glove is always way out in front—as far out in front as anybody I've ever seen. That helps him adjust to tricky little hops. You have to trust your eyes. If your hands are out in front and you can see the ball and the glove, the eyes are going to tell your brain, which is still the world's fastest computer, what to do and help you adjust. So if your hands always stay in proper position, you're much more likely to catch a ball that takes a bad hop.

◆ ◆

CAL'S CORNER

When you're teaching young infielders and you're talking about getting wide, make sure they understand what your terminology is and what *wide* means. It's a personal preference. It could be as narrow as your shoulders. It could be a lot wider. But ordinarily I would use the player's shoulder width as the starting point.

THROWING AFTER THE CATCH

Now let's talk about making the throw after fielding a routine ground ball. We've caught the ball out in front in the center of our body, so the next step is a simple technique of bringing the hands into the center of the body. Once this is accomplished, we need to shuffle our feet toward the target (never crossing or hopping). By shuffling our feet toward the target, we create momentum and allow our shoulders to stay horizontal to the ground. This is important because our front shoulder should be pointed directly toward the target. By crossing your feet or hopping, the front shoulder has a ten-

After catching a ground ball it's important to generate momentum toward the target and follow the throw.

dency to point upward. With a consistent shuffle toward the target, pointing the front shoulder and releasing the ball, the infielder will find it easy to allow his momentum to follow the throw. Those are the three key components of an accurate throw: creating momentum toward your target, pointing your front shoulder toward your target while throwing, and using your momentum to follow the throw.

By shuffling your feet toward your target you can close the distance between you and the target. That's less distance that you have to throw the ball. Wouldn't you rather throw it 60 feet than 70 feet? You're going to be more accurate on a shorter throw. It's also going to be less wear and tear on your arm if you move your feet properly. It requires less effort, and the ball is going to go exactly where it should go. Derek Jeter is a great example. Watch him play shortstop. Ground ball to him, no one on. He catches the ball and throws it to the first baseman for the out. By the time he gets the ball back from the first baseman, he's standing on the infield grass. He started at normal depth. The ball was hit hard at him. He might've come in one or two steps to catch it. But he finishes on the infield grass. The two things that he does: He really gets momentum toward the target once he catches the ball, and after he throws it, he follows the throw.

The four-seam grip.

Keep in mind that every throw made by an infielder—or, for that matter, every throw made by any position player—should be made with the four-seam grip, across the seams. Why? Because the ball carries and it also goes straight. We're not trying to trick the first baseman if we're infielders. We're not trying to trick the infielders if we're outfielders. We're trying to throw the ball straight.

Infielders should get in the habit of throwing the ball at the middle of the target player's chest. That's where it's easiest to catch.

BILL'S BALL GAME

Throwing the ball is a big part of the game of baseball. Playing catch is a part of all practices, but kids get bored quickly with just playing catch. Think of throwing in terms of target practice. Dad always used to say, "The better we play catch, the better we play baseball." This is a theme we come back to over and over again. When we play defense, we're essentially playing a game of catch.

A good starting point for kids playing catch is to have them take one step toward the target as they throw. It's not much more effort than if they were just standing flat-footed. But all of a sudden they've got a little giddyup on their throw. So every time they're playing catch, have them step toward the target, point their front shoulder, and make the throw.

We've all seen kids lined up playing catch before the game starts. And they're just lobbing it, and the balls are rattling against the chain link fence behind them, which is the worst sound in all of baseball. When that ball hits that fence, that ball did not go where it was supposed to go.

I always say that I can take sixteen kids, put eight of them on one side and eight on the other. I tell them I'm going to pitch in the game. I'm going to throw every ball 60 miles an hour, right down Broadway. Let them play the game. But before the game I'm going to watch those first eight kids play catch, and I'm going to watch the other eight kids play catch. And based on that I'll tell you who's going to win the game. I won't watch any kid take batting practice. The eight kids who throw the ball back and forth better with each other are going to win the game. It usually comes down to that in the game of baseball: who plays catch better.

BALLS HIT TO EITHER SIDE: THE CROSSOVER STEP

The routine ground ball, one hit directly at the infielder, should be the easiest one to catch, because the ready position provides for an easy transition into the proper fielding position. The infielder simply has to get his rear end down and his hands out in front. But what if the ball's hit to your side?

Let's start with an example: If the ball is hit to your right, you use the crossover step to move toward it. You simply cross over with the foot furthest from the ball (in this case your left) as your first step. This is the most efficient way to move laterally on the baseball field. (Right now we're focusing on getting in front of the ball; the backhand will come into play later.) The ball is hit three steps to your right, you see the ball, you read the ball, and you cross over. As you cross over you're pivoting on your right foot. The crossover step is simply that: Your left foot crosses over the right foot to get going. When you do this, the focus should be on maintaining the proper footwork. It's better to take a split second to read that the ball is to your right and make sure that your footwork is properly done. That'll help as you get older and play more baseball. The crossover step will become second nature and the movement will be even more efficient.

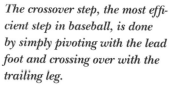

The crossover step, the most efficient step in baseball, is done by simply pivoting with the lead foot and crossing over with the trailing leg.

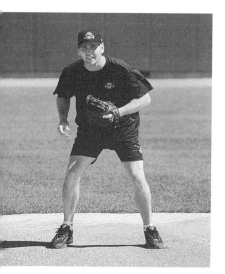  

⊘ Don't pick up your lead foot and move it out wider and then put it back down. That's a wasted movement—by the time you do that you could've done the crossover step.

Good lateral movement will allow you to get in front of balls that you normally wouldn't. Once you get in front of the ball the fundamentals of fielding and throwing come into play.

BACKHANDS

The backhand is generally a more difficult play than the basic ground ball or the ground ball hit to the forehand side. The biggest problem that young infielders have with the backhand is that they try to catch the ball behind them. The backhand is still caught out in front of the body. We never catch the ball behind us in this game unless it's an extreme case.

The three principles of fielding a ground ball still apply to the backhand. With a backhand the wide base gets a little wider than when a ball is hit right at you. With that in mind, it stands to reason that if your base is wider, your rear end is automatically going to be lower to the ground. This will allow your glove to be out in front of the body.

There are two types of backhand plays: one in which the right foot is the lead foot and one in which the left foot is the lead foot. Let's first talk about using the right foot as the lead. This is a play in which you can't comfortably get in front of the ball, so in a sense you're going to take your right foot into the path of the baseball. When you do this you've created a wider base. And by collapsing the trailing leg you've gotten your rear end lower to the ground, creating a lunge position and allowing you to have the glove out in front of your body directly between the ball and the foot. Once you catch the ball you should bring it into the center of your body, allowing the basic throwing principles to take over.

When the ball is hit further to the backhand side, it becomes necessary to use the left foot as the lead. Using the left foot as the lead allows you to have more reach. The same basic principles for the right-footed backhand still apply. The main difference is that the ball is played outside of the lead foot instead of even with it. Everything else is essentially the same.

There are two ways to catch a backhand: right foot out (A) and left foot out (B). Both are okay, and in both cases we catch the ball out front.

A lot of young infielders attempting the left-footed backhand want to play the ball behind them. You shouldn't do that. At the most extreme case you may catch the ball even with the foot, but never behind it. The backhand is a one-handed play. Catch the ball first, then bring it to the center of your body to set up for the throw.

BILL'S BALL GAME

I call the right-footed backhand play the "routine" backhand play at the big league level. What I mean by that is if I'm playing shortstop and Kenny Lofton is hitting and he hits a hard ball two or three steps to my right, if I try to get in front of that ball and catch it with my momentum going toward the left field foul line, I can't recover in time to throw him out. But I'm confident enough in my backhand that I take my right foot to the baseball. I'm wide, and I'm low enough that I can catch and throw all in one motion.

TROUBLESHOOTING THE BACKHAND

When attempting backhands, young infielders, even if they're in a position to catch the ball out in front, often want to take the glove away from the ball too quickly. Gloves are designed well enough these days that the backhand is a one-handed play, period. Catch the ball first and bring it into the center of the body, but don't be in too much of a hurry.

Another big problem with younger players on the backhand is balls bouncing off the wrist and forearm. That means the infielder is trying to catch the ball behind him. If you set up with your glove behind your body, you're going to see the forearm and wrist come into play a lot more often than if you catch the ball out in front. If you're playing catch in the backyard and the ball is thrown to your backhand side, you don't reach behind to catch the ball. You reach out and turn the glove to the backhand position. The same thing should happen on a ground ball hit to your backhand side.

CAL'S CORNER

The backhand shouldn't be something that you're intimidated by. In the first few years in the minor leagues, most players, including myself, have much more confidence in getting in front of the ball, which results in taking their body position away from first base, making it more difficult to make a good throw to the bag. So it's useful for coaches to introduce both backhand plays in the form of drills; that'll get the infielders' confidence level up and ultimately help them overall. The sooner you get to understand that the backhand is a great tool to put into your fielding arsenal, the better off you'll be.

◆ ◆

THROWING OFF THE BACKHAND

When using the backhand you have the ability to stop your momentum from continuing away from your target. After successfully catching the ball with the backhand, the infielder should use either foot to stop his momentum and then push off to create momentum back toward the target.

After fielding the ground ball, bring your hands to the center of your body. Don't sweep your hands to the side in a circular motion in an attempt to get rid of the ball more quickly. This can throw the body out of whack and cause a bad throw. Make a little turn toward first base and make sure your shoulders remain parallel to the ground while throwing.

An infielder trying to throw too hard may point his shoulder up and then throw high, or pull down at the last second and throw low.

FOREHAND PLAYS

As with the backhand, you should use the crossover step when pursuing the ball on a forehand play. The goal is to get to a position where the left foot is closest to the baseball. That's going to enable you to reach out and catch the ball in front of your body. Some extreme cases may arise in which this is not the case. Again, if you can't get in front of a ground ball, this becomes a one-handed play. You really have to concentrate on keeping your eyes on the ball and the glove. The glove has to be out in front. Generally the forehand is an easier play than the backhand. The same principles apply.

A forehand play on the run can sometimes be extreme, but you should still try to catch the ball out in front.

THROWING OFF THE FOREHAND

We sometimes see young infielders, especially going up the middle from shortstop or going toward their left from third, catching the ball and throwing it with their momentum going toward right-centerfield. They don't get their bodies turned and moving toward first base. Once you catch the ball, half the play is done. The rest of the job is to make a good, accurate throw. And the best way to do that is to get your momentum going toward the target. You have to make a concerted effort to get your front shoulder pointed toward that target. Once the throw is made, take an extra step or two in the same direction. This will increase the accuracy of the throw.

◆ ◆ ◆ ◆ ◆ ◆ ◆ ◆ ◆ ◆ ◆ ◆ ◆ ◆ ◆ ◆ ◆ ◆ ◆ ◆

CAL'S CORNER

When I think of throwing off the forehand, I remember two ways that I liked to execute this play. This is probably a little advanced, in application if not in writing, but I just couldn't resist. On a ball to my left that I would field even with or slightly ahead of my left foot, I would make the throw a more conventional way, by just rotating my body and my left shoulder toward first. If I had to extend and if I caught the ball behind me (on a forehand this sometimes happens), I would spin my whole body around in a circle and then deliver the ball to first. I found that there was a point and an angle from which it was difficult to simply rotate my body toward first and still make a good throw. But by spinning and using the momentum of my reach for the ball, I could get a lot on the throw. It's a little tricky, because when you spin it's difficult to pick up your target. But give the spin a try in practice; you might like it.

◆ ◆ ◆ ◆ ◆ ◆ ◆ ◆ ◆ ◆ ◆ ◆ ◆ ◆ ◆ ◆ ◆ ◆ ◆ ◆

PLAYING FIRST BASE

When no one's on base, the first baseman has the same responsibilities as any other infielder: He must be ready to field a ground ball if it's hit in his direction. A misconception is that because a first baseman's glove is different, things are done differently at that position. Not true. Catching a ground ball is catching a ground ball, and the same fundamentals apply to the first baseman that apply to any other infielder.

When the ball is hit to another infielder, the priority changes. At the younger ages it's more important for a first baseman to play more shallow, because it's even more crucial for him to be able to receive throws from other infielders than it is for him to field ground balls himself. We still don't want the first baseman to play on the bag, but at the younger ages it's better to err by positioning the first baseman too close to the bag instead of too far away.

When a ground ball is hit to another infielder, the first baseman must get to the bag early and set up to be a good target. A good target is one that is stationary, square to the infielder who's making the throw, and big (not squatting or scrunching down).

It's important for the first baseman to get to the bag early and be a good target, square to the infielder who's throwing him the ball.

⊘ The first baseman should never set up by crouching down low.

A first baseman should set up with the heel of his throwing-side foot on the center of the inside part of the base. We've all seen a young kid stand right on top of the bag, and then a big collision occurs at first base. So start with your heel on the bag, right in the middle of it. It gives you room to play. Slide your foot on the bag for throws up or down the line. You want to be square to the player who's throwing the ball. It's a bad feeling if you're the shortstop and you go into the hole and backhand a ball, then look up across the diamond and see the first baseman off the bag. Where are you going to have a tendency to throw it? Where you last saw him. So it's important for the first baseman to get to the bag as early as he can to be a good target.

The first baseman should then see the ball coming across the infield, making sure he has determined the flight of the ball before committing his stretch. The stretch should result

The first baseman's glove and glove-side foot should work in tandem (left), not separately (⊘ right).

from the first baseman seeing the flight of the ball and then taking his glove-hand foot and glove to the baseball in tandem. A stretch should not necessarily be defined by going toward the player who threw the ball, but by the glove-hand foot and the glove going directly toward the baseball. In simple terms, you can stretch up the line toward home plate, in toward the fielder who threw the ball, or up the line toward the right field corner. If you're able to catch the ball at the same time your glove-hand foot touches the ground, this will prove that you've seen the ball cross the diamond and have taken the proper steps to catch it. Getting off the base and blocking or catching a bad throw is better than missing the ball altogether.

So the two golden rules of first-base play are:

1) If the ball isn't hit to you, get to the bag and set up as soon as you can to be a good target.
2) Don't stretch too soon.

You want to be ready for a bad throw, but a lot of first basemen think getting ready for a bad throw means hunkering down. You want to stay up, in an athletic stance, and take your glove-side foot to the baseball. Pretend there's a cable between your glove-hand wrist and your knee on your glove side, and wherever that wrist goes, it's going to pull your knee with it. You want to read the ball as it's coming across the diamond. Ideally the ball should hit your glove at the same time your foot hits the ground.

A lot of times we see young first basemen already stretching before the throw is even made. If you do that, then you have to retool before you can go anywhere. And the only throw you're going to catch in that position is a good one. That's not your ready position. As a first baseman, you don't know where the infielder is going to throw it. You hope he's going to throw it to the right spot, but you have to be ready to move right or left. So you're set up, just like a fielder getting ready for the ball to be hit. You're square to where the ball is coming from, in a ready position.

For some reason people often want to make the first baseman the big guy with bad hands who can hit for power, but in reality the first baseman handles more balls than anyone on the field except the catcher. So the better your first baseman handles balls thrown by the other infielders, the better your team will be as a whole.

When you're playing first base on a 60-foot diamond, think about all the abilities of your pitcher. The deeper you play and the further you play off the line, the more responsibility you're putting on your pitcher to cover first base. As you go up the ladder, the pitcher's responsibility is to cover first on any ground ball hit to the right side. When the field is a little bit shorter, pitchers don't always have the ability to do that. So on a smaller diamond you should be concerned about playing your position like the other infielders and not thinking about the pitcher taking responsibility for covering first base.

◆ ◆

CAL'S CORNER

A first baseman's responsibility for receiving throws from his infielders should outweigh ranging far to his right and fielding ground balls. It is an added value if he can do both, but his ability to receive throws properly will make his team better. So if you're going to make a mistake as a first baseman, you never want it to be arriving late to the bag. If you need to sacrifice a little range to make sure you get there on time, that's what you should do.

◆ ◆

DOUBLE PLAY DEPTH

When we talk about the infield at double play depth, we're referring to the middle infielders. In order to consider double play depth, these conditions must exist: There must be a runner on first base and fewer than two outs. Let's throw out all the formulas for where to play. If, for example, you're playing second base, you know that you have to come up and over toward second base to complete the double play if a ground ball is hit. Now, look at your off-infielders—the shortstop and the third baseman. These are the guys who are going to be involved on a double play ball. Ask yourself, "If that ball is hit hard—a sharp, two-hop ground ball to my shortstop—can I get to second base in my proper setup position and be a target for my shortstop?" If the ball is a hard-hit two-hopper to shortstop, if it's a firm two-hopper—not a rocket—and you can't get there, if you're still on the move when he's ready to throw to you, then automatically you should tell yourself that your double play depth is not correct. You need to move in and over a little bit.

There's a comfort zone for each infielder who plays the middle. One player's double play depth might be three steps in and three steps over. Another guy's might be two in and two over, so you must ask yourself as a middle infielder, "Can I get to second base, set up in the right manner, and be a good target for my shortstop if he gets a firm two-hopper hit to him?" That's your simple formula for double play depth.

As a second baseman you're going to take a direct route to the bag, so when you get there you're in perfect position to receive the throw. You're going to put your left foot on the bag, and your shoulders should be square to the shortstop or third baseman, whichever one is throwing to you. You're ready, anticipating a bad throw, because if you anticipate a bad throw and you get a good throw, it's a piece of cake. But if you do it the opposite way—you're anticipating a good throw as opposed to a bad throw—you become surprised if it's in the dirt and therefore you can't react to the ball as well.

If you use the proper footwork, you'll align yourself to throw to first base in the right manner, with your front shoulder pointing toward first base as you throw there.

On the shortstop side the same principles apply. You need to get to the base to record the out. You need to get there early just like the second baseman does. You have a little more leeway than he does because your momentum is toward first base, where you're going to throw the ball. We're not telling you to get there late, but you can see based on all the principles we're talking about that you're coming in a direct line and you don't have to worry about changing your momentum. What you do have to worry about is slowing down as you approach second base. You want to put your right foot on the bag.

The reason you want to get there early is so you can help out on a bad throw and you can get your footwork crisp so you can take your left foot to the ball. Taking your left foot to the ball puts your body in a position to throw. Don't be lazy getting to the bag; if you're moving at all and there's a bad throw, you're not in a position to react. If you catch it with two hands, you're not wasting any effort or any time. You can transfer the ball to your bare hand and make the throw much more quickly. The advantages of having your bare hand and glove hand together are that it shortens the turn, it makes the transition from your glove to your hand easier, and it gets you in a good position to make a strong, accurate throw.

The shortstop should look at the second baseman and at the first baseman. If there's a man on first and no one else on, the first baseman is going to be holding the runner. So it might be a little bit tighter for you. Look at the second baseman and say to yourself, "If there's a two-hopper hit right at my second baseman, can I get to second, set up in the proper manner, and be a good, stationary target for my second baseman?"

Remember that defense is two parts: catching and throwing. If we're having a catch in the backyard, we're not throwing to a guy who's running post patterns or curl patterns.

We're playing catch with someone whose shoulders are square to us. We see his chest, and that's what we want to throw to. The double play is no different. If we eliminate throwing to people when they're moving, we're going to be a better ball club because we're going to play catch better.

EXECUTING THE DOUBLE PLAY: SECOND BASEMAN

Now you know what your double play depth is. You feel comfortable that you can get there when balls are hit sharply to the third baseman or the shortstop. So how do you get to the base and how do you set up? First and foremost, you make a straight line from your position to the bag. Eliminate rounding the base and any other path that deviates from going straight to it. The quicker you get to the base, the quicker you can set up and the easier it is for your teammate to throw to a stationary target.

As a second baseman, you're going to get to the bag and put your left foot on it. You're waiting and your shoulders are square to the fielder who's throwing to you. Don't straddle the base.

Wherever the throw comes from, if it's a perfect throw right over the middle of the second-base bag, you can do a number of things. You can take your right foot and simply walk toward where the throw came from, catch it, plant your left foot, and make a throw to first base. If the throw is to the left field side of the bag, you take your right foot toward the ball. Your right foot always goes toward the baseball. The left foot goes to the bag, then you check to see the flight of the ball. If the throw is toward the first-base bag, you can cross over with your right foot and catch it. What that does is ensure that every time you take your right foot to the baseball, it takes the center of your body to the ball. That's where you want to catch the ball, because ultimately you're going to bring it back to the center of your body when you make the throw to first base.

We know we've said this before, but it's worth repeating: Second basemen need to get to the bag early—as quickly as possible on a straight line. Anticipate a bad throw, because if it's a good throw you can do anything with your right foot. You can walk to it or you can kind of step back, but the left foot goes to the bag and the right foot goes to the baseball every time when you're playing second base.

Keep in mind as a second baseman that there are different ways to turn the double play. It's pretty much dictated by where the throw is coming to you. If you get to the bag with your left foot to the base and your right foot goes toward the ball and the throw is up the line, you cross over the bag, stepping to the ball with your right foot. If the ball is behind the bag on the left field side, your right foot goes out toward the ball so that you're using the bag as your friend to turn the double play. If it's a perfect throw, you can do one of two things: You can step across the bag toward the ball, or if the throw has good pace on it, you can just step back.

The three basic ways to turn a double play by the second baseman are:

1) Go across the bag to the ball.
2) Take the right foot to the left field side,
   using the bag as your friend.
3) Step back.

These three different methods of turning the double play allow the second baseman to give the baserunner a different look every time, but the throw actually dictates what the second baseman does on his double play. If he's in proper position he can handle any throw. Remember, get there early and set up as a stationary target, taking the left foot to the base and the right foot to the ball.

EXECUTING THE DOUBLE PLAY: SHORTSTOP

The shortstop needs to get to the bag early. There are two basic approaches to this. We're going to start with the most basic way, for the younger ages. Put your right foot on the bag, with your shoulders square to your second baseman, where the throw is coming from. Once you're square to that player and you give him a good target, you read where the throw is going, because that dictates your movements as an infielder. If it's a perfect throw, you take your left foot toward the ball, which takes the center of your body to the ball.

Shortstops have to be conscious about getting their feet and front shoulder pointed back toward first base once they receive the feed from the second baseman. When you catch the ball, you should be square to the second baseman, so then you have to move your feet, and there's a long way to travel. Once you catch the ball, you have to concentrate on swinging your feet around and getting in line to first base to make the throw. Moving your feet will also point your front shoulder in the right direction.

What happens when the shortstop is receiving the double play feed from the first baseman in a first-and-second situation with one or none out? If the first baseman is behind the runner, the shortstop is going to get to the second-base bag in the same manner that he did when he was receiving the ball from the second baseman. Now, if there's a man just on first base, and the first baseman is holding the runner on and he bounces off and is inside of the runner, the shortstop can then get to the inside of the bag and place his left foot on second base. When the throw arrives, he catches the ball and takes a step toward first. If the throw happens to take him to the outfield side and across the runner's path, then he can move his feet and take his left foot to the ball, using his right foot to touch second base before getting his feet back into proper position to throw to first.

THE PIVOT

The pivot man on the double play should always try to use two hands. Middle infielders should get into the practice of using two hands and catching the ball out in front so they can see the ball entering their glove. The reason we use two hands is that we're going to have to make a transfer and a throw. So instead of reaching out with one hand, then bringing that hand to meet the other, it makes sense that if you reach out with both hands and catch the ball, the transfer is going to be easier for you to make. When receiving a throw at second, even for the third out of an inning, the second baseman and shortstop should get in the habit of positioning themselves as if they're starting a double play by getting there early, being a good target for the infield partner, and catching the ball out in front with two hands.

On the pivot the second baseman's setup should be with the left foot on the bag. By taking his right foot to the baseball, he'll always be in proper position to make the throw to first base.

The shortstop's pivot setup should be right foot on the bag, and take the left foot to the ball. Here the shortstop has to make a concerted effort to get his front shoulder pointed toward the target.

THE UNDERHAND FLIP

The underhand flip is an important part of infield defense that's often taken for granted. It's used by all infielders, even the catcher. At the highest level the underhand flip can be used by the middle infielders to start two thirds of all double plays. How does that relate to youth baseball? Well, it may not start the 6-4-3 or the 4-6-3 double play at the twelve-year-old level, but it can be used as a valuable tool in eliminating errors that occur when trying to record a force-out at second base.

Most errors occur at second base at the youth level because one of two things happens: Either it's a bad overhand feed that's thrown too hard, or a middle infielder gets to the bag too late. When it's a combination of both, the end result is not good. By developing the proper technique of the underhand flip, errors can be eliminated at the youth level, and the better you do your job to start the double play with the underhand flip at the higher levels, the better chance you have of completing the double play.

The mechanics of the underhand flip can be broken down into three parts after the ball is fielded:

1) Stay low and take your momentum toward the target by using your feet.
2) Flip the ball with a stiff wrist and your hand behind the ball, leaving your hand at the target's face level.
3) Follow the ball.

Creating momentum can be done in two ways. The easiest way for younger players to do it is by shuffling their feet toward the intended target. A more advanced and the most efficient way to do it is by using a crossover step and exploding toward the target.

The shortstop has the advantage of being almost open to

The underhand flip can be a valuable weapon for starting double plays at the highest levels. At the younger levels it can be an effective way to get the force-out at second base.

second base to begin with. Whether the shortstop is shuffling or using the crossover step, the underhand flip should feel more natural. Derek Jeter has the best fundamentals in the game with the underhand flip; watch the momentum he generates toward the bag. The second baseman's underhand flip will be slightly more difficult and uncomfortable. The tendency of a young second baseman, even if the footwork is done correctly, is to bring the ball from in front of his body all the way to a point behind his body before executing the flip. The key here is to try to get the second baseman to flip the ball from about where it was caught. If the ball is caught out in front, it makes sense to flip it right from that spot. This may result in an awkward feeling for the second baseman until this technique is mastered.

From either shortstop or second base, the principles are the same. You have to create momentum to the target, flip the ball and leave the hand to the face, and follow the flip. The underhand flip is a tool that can be used at the highest level, but it's a fundamental skill that should be introduced even to the youngest players.

When you're covering the bag on a steal, the setup should be one where you straddle the bag.

COVERING THE BASE ON A STEAL

The most important thing for an infielder covering the base on a steal is to get to the base early. This is similar to the responsibility of the first baseman on a ground ball. When you get there early, you provide a target for the catcher and you allow yourself to pick up the flight of the ball at the earliest point. By picking up the ball early you get a better read on the throw.

Straddle the base. The runner has to get to the bag to be safe. By straddling the bag you put yourself in a position where the runner has to come to you. You're also in the best position to administer a tag. As with receiving every other throw, assume it's going to be a bad throw. If you're ready for a bad throw, you can better react, and if the throw is a good one, the play is that much easier. If the throw is low and up the line, leave the straddle position and take a route in front of the runner to catch the ball.

⊘ By being in front of the base and not straddling it you'll catch the ball sooner, but your arm can't move as fast as the ball.

Let the ball travel to you. Don't reach up in front to catch the ball. This is one of the rare times when you don't catch the ball out front. The reason you let the ball travel is simple. The ball is traveling much faster than you can move it with your glove. Imagine a short race between the ball traveling to the base by itself and you holding the ball in your glove in front of the base and taking it as fast as you can to the bag. It's a small thing, but the difference between being out and being safe can be very small. Take every advantage available to you.

When applying a tag, put the tag straight down and straight back up. You want to avoid any chance of the ball being knocked out of your glove by the slide. If the throw is high and up the line, take a route behind the runner to attempt a catch and a possible tag. Remember that if you're late to the base, everything but a perfect throw is made more difficult. Remember your responsibility to the catcher and the team. By catching a bad throw or blocking a bad throw, or especially turning an errant throw into an out, you're helping the team.

RUNDOWNS

A rundown occurs when a runner is caught between two bases. The goal of a rundown is to get the runner moving full speed in one direction and to make one throw. The rundown starts with the infielder taking the ball out of his glove and

It's important in a rundown to get the ball out of the glove early and get it in a throwing position.

with the ball in his throwing hand, in a position ready to throw, running directly at the runner, forcing him to commit to one direction full speed. Once the infielder gets the runner running in one direction at full speed, the other infielder calls for the ball by saying, "Now!" The throw is one of touch. The infielder flips the ball to his teammate chest high. He catches the ball first and makes the tag second. It sounds simple enough, but as usual there's more to it than there seems.

As we said, a rundown starts because the baserunner is caught between bases. But where he is varies depending upon the situation. A runner picked off is in a different position than a runner trying to take an extra base. And not all pick-offs are the same. A base stealer who starts back on a pickoff is different from one who leaves early and is caught in the middle. The bottom line is that it's 90 feet between bases and the runner could be anywhere within those 90 feet. So it's important how the rundown is started. There are some fundamentals important to all rundowns:

- Always run with the ball in your throwing hand and in a position to throw. You need to be ready to throw at all times.
- No pump-faking. By having the ball in the ready-to-throw position the other infielder can see the ball and time his move. You don't want to deceive your infielders.

Once you get the runner running hard in one direction, you'll be able to record the out with a dartlike toss .

- When you get the runner moving, it's important to run directly at him, as fast and as under control as you can. The runner has no choice but to move in the direction you choose.
- Generally speaking, it's good to use the full 90 feet between bases. In order to get the runner moving full speed in one direction, you need enough distance to accomplish your task. The reason it's necessary to get the runner moving full speed in one direction is to prevent the runner from changing direction. It's virtually impossible, no matter how fast the runner, for him to stop from full speed and go in the other direction before he can be tagged out.
- One throw is ideal. The more throws, the greater the chance of error. Even in the big leagues, where based on skill level alone the rundown should be an automatic out, sometimes it's messed up. That usually happens because of too many throws.
- To minimize the number of throws and in order to get the rundown started most efficiently, it's not necessarily true that you must run the runner back to the base from which he came. That theory is based on the notion that if you mess up the rundown, the runner is back where he started. The theory that if a runner is caught in a rundown he should be out is a better one. It then becomes a matter of execution of the rundown itself. The start of the rundown depends on the position of the runner in the baseline; to keep the number of throws to a minimum, it makes sense to have the option of running in either direction.
- Remember that the key to a successful rundown is getting set up to be able to run the runner hard in one direction. Whereas one throw is ideal, sometimes it takes the first throw to get things set up.

FLY BALL PRIORITIES

The defense is made up of nine players with gloves on their hands. Each of these players has specific responsibilities. These responsibilities collectively define the positions. Sometimes the responsibilities overlap. Communication and familiarity with the other fielders help in dealing with these overlaps, but some general guidelines will give a greater understanding and will allow the whole defense to execute at a higher level.

When a fly ball comes down at exactly one of the positions, it's easy to understand who should catch that ball. But what happens when it comes down between two or more positions?

A basic rule is that a fly ball is easier to catch if the fielder is coming in on the ball. The play is in front of you, and the ball is easier to judge and to track. It makes sense that if two or more players are going after a fly ball, the one who should have the priority is the one coming in on the ball. With this simple rule in mind, let's take a look at the field and identify some areas that overlap:

◆ **A fly ball to shallow left field.** The shortstop goes back and the left fielder is coming in. If the left fielder can catch the ball, he calls off the shortstop and makes the play. The job of the shortstop is to go after the ball until he's called off by the left fielder. It's very important for the left fielder to call off the shortstop on every ball he can catch. If he doesn't feel he can call off the shortstop, then he should give the shortstop the opportunity to catch the ball.

◆ **A fly ball behind third base and a little down the left field line.** The shortstop has the better angle and the responsibility to call off the third baseman. If the shortstop can make the play, he must call off the third baseman. If he can't get to the ball, then he should give the third baseman a chance to catch it. If this play also involves the left fielder, he has priority over the shortstop and the third baseman.

◆ **A fly ball between the catcher and third baseman.** It's a much easier play for the third baseman coming in on the ball. If he can make the play, he should call off the catcher. The catcher should pursue the ball until he's called off.

◆ **A fly ball in the middle of the infield.** The shortstop has priority over all the other infielders. If the shortstop calls the ball, then it's his.

◆ **A fly ball between the center fielder and left fielder.** The center fielder has priority over all outfielders. The left fielder goes after every ball until he's called off by the center fielder. The same goes for the right fielder.

◆ **A fly ball between the shortstop and second baseman.** Again, the shortstop has priority over all infielders. Good judgment is required because the second baseman has the same angles and position on the field as the shortstop. If the second baseman has the easier play, the shortstop should let him have the ball.

As you can see there's a commonsense approach when more than one defender is going after a fly ball, but there are also specific priorities. Here's a summary of the rules:

- The shortstop has priority over all infielders.
- The middle infielders have priority over the corner infielders.
- The corner infielders have priority over the catcher and the pitcher.
- The outfielders have priority over the infielders.
- The center fielder has priority over the left fielder and right fielder.

CUTOFFS AND RELAYS

A cutoff is different from a relay. They're usually grouped together and often thought of as the same. A cutoff is essentially intercepting the ball—stopping a throw before it gets to its destination. There are many reasons to stop the flight of the ball or cut the ball: The throw is off-line or late. To keep the other runners from advancing to the next base. To keep the double play in order. To minimize a potential big inning. If the runner falls down.

A relay is not stopping the throw from its destination but helping it get there. As a relay man your job is to keep the ball going to its target. A long throw from the fence in centerfield needs to be helped by the relay man to get the ball to home plate.

It's important for the relay man to be a good target. He needs to move into position to catch the throw from the outfield and throw to the next base.

The confusion lies in the situation. A cutoff man and a relay man can be one and the same. The situation and the player making the throw dictate what your role will be. There are some general guidelines in which we can operate. If an outfielder is throwing to a base and it's within his range (his arm strength), then the infielder between the outfielder making the throw and the target becomes the cutoff man. If the throw is outside his range, then the fielder in between could be a relay man or a cutoff man. So arm strength has a lot to do with cutoffs and relays.

For the purpose of understanding the differences, let's look at cutoffs and relays at the big league level. Arm strength becomes less of an issue because everyone can execute all the throws. It then becomes a matter of strategy and probability. These things are usually factored in ahead of time, before the play begins. In the big leagues if the outfielder has a direct chance to throw a runner out at second, third, or home, the fielder in between becomes a cutoff man. In a rare situation an infielder might relay successfully, but generally there wouldn't be enough time to relay the ball and throw the runner out. The only time you become a relay man is on an extra-base hit when there might be a play at third or home.

Once you've determined which role you'll play, a cutoff man or a relay man, positioning becomes critical. If you're a cutoff man, you need to position yourself to manage the throw. The cutoff man's position should be deeper (closer to the target base) because his responsibility is to cut off the throw, not to relay it. The deeper position allows you to get a longer look at the throw. This enables you to determine better if the throw is off-line or if it's strong enough to reach its target. An advanced benefit is that it allows you to calculate the runner's speed against the flight of the ball to determine if the throw will actually get there in time for the out. By assuming a deeper position you have a greater vision of the field and the other baserunners.

Sometimes the position of the cutoff man is taught by determining that if the throw hits the cutoff man in the chest it should be a perfect one-hop throw to its target. This is an excellent rule of thumb when instructing players age sixteen and under. Players over sixteen have developed their arm strength and should understand where they need to bounce the ball in order to make a perfect one-hop throw. The cutoff man should no longer be a reference for the outfielder. The outfielder should pick a spot on the ground at which to aim to make that perfect one-hop throw. The cutoff man should still assume a position in line with the throw where he can manage that throw. The outfielder's arm strength, the game situation, and other baserunners are all factors that can help determine the cutoff man's position. As a cutoff man you want to position yourself where your options are all in front of you. Take a position where the outfielder can't overthrow you without also overthrowing his target.

If you're a relay man, you should choose a position that allows you to make a quick and strong relay to the base. You need to get to your spot early, be a big target, and generate momentum in the direction you're throwing. A perfect throw to a relay man is chest- to head-high. With this in mind you need to choose a position where the outfielder can deliver the ball chest- to head-high. Determining the outfielder's arm strength as well as your own is important in choosing a relay position. The reason a chest-high to head-high throw is perfect is that it allows you the chance to create momentum while you're tracking the ball and it's easier to make a fast and clean transfer from your glove to your throwing hand.

In most relay situations there's a trailer. A trailer is simply a safety valve for the relay. He's Plan B. If there's a line drive to the gap in left-center with a man on first base, a relay has to be set up to throw the ball to home plate in the event the runner on first tries to score. The shortstop would go out into shallow left-center and line up the throw home. The second baseman would trail the play, taking a position behind the shortstop and also in line with home plate. His position should be based on the assumption that the throw is going to be a bad throw to the shortstop. If the throw is high and goes over the head of the relay man, the trailer should be in position so that it becomes a perfect throw to him. If the throw is low and will short-hop the relay man, the trailer should be in a position so that it becomes a perfect throw to him on the long hop. In the second example the relay man should recognize the bad low throw and let it go to the trailer.

You've probably heard the expression "Never overthrow the cutoff man." That's true, but as we've learned there's a difference between a cutoff man and a relay man. It's okay to overthrow a relay man. As a matter of fact, it's encouraged. The outfielder should aim on the high side when throwing to the relay man. As we stated earlier, the ball can be relayed faster and stronger if the relay man can receive it chest- to head-high. And an overthrow of the relay man is a perfect throw to the trailer.

Let's go back to the expression "Never overthrow the cutoff man." This is a true statement with respect to a cutoff man specifically. An overthrow allows other baserunners the opportunity to advance. People immediately focus on the outfielder's throw as the source of that mistake. But that's not always the case. It's the cutoff man's responsibility not to allow the other runners to advance a base. It's his job to manage the throw, and it's his job to assume the right position and avoid an overthrow.

CAL'S CORNER

The subject of cutoffs and relays, and specifically the differences between them, gets me jazzed. This part of the game is so simple, but it can get very complicated as you climb the ladder to the higher levels. At the introductory level, cutoffs and relays are necessary simply to get the ball from one location to another. At the advanced level, they're more about strategy.

Mom and Dad (second from right) taught us a lot about baseball and life, and always encouraged us to share what

On an All-Star baseball tour of Japan in 1996 I had the pleasure of sharing the shortstop duties with Alex Rodriguez. During this trip I had the chance to talk about many of the more advanced concepts of shortstop with Alex. When it's all said and done, Alex will be viewed as the best shortstop in the history of baseball. Physically, he's big and strong with great agility and speed. Armed with these tools, there are virtually no limitations to his potential on the baseball field. At that time the things that I had over young Alex were experience and a greater understanding of the game. It was my goal to give him the benefits of that experience.

One very memorable interaction took place in the Tokyo Dome after an early practice. Alex was interested in positioning for the different cutoff and relay responsibilities of the shortstop. We had the whole field at our disposal, so I used it as one big classroom. Diagrams on a sheet of paper can help get a concept across, but being able to show the exact positioning points on the field deepens understanding. So Alex and I walked all over the artificial turf in the dome, talking over the finer points of positioning for cutoffs and

PHOTO COPYRIGHT © HEATHER HALL

we know, be it with major leaguers such as Alex Rodriguez (two left photos) or young players like Ryan (right).

relays. One of the best things about Alex is that he has this incredible zest to learn. He's like a sponge, soaking up everything he can. He asks questions all the time and loves to talk baseball. As we were discussing the more advanced points in our own little world, we didn't notice that some members of the Japanese media were watching. I received a lot of positive comments for taking the time to teach Alex, but in reality I was just doing what Dad did his whole life, passing on the craft. To Dad it was about honoring and improving the game. And sharing what you know is one of the best ways.

◆ ◆ ◆ ◆ ◆ ◆ ◆ ◆ ◆ ◆ ◆ ◆ ◆ ◆ ◆ ◆ ◆ ◆

PERFECT PRACTICE MAKES PERFECT: THROWING DRILL

We use this drill for players of all ages to reinforce the concept of generating momentum toward the target and following the throw. The drill simulates a third-to-second force-out. The players line up single file (remember to have the second player in line give the first player plenty of room) facing a coach who's standing ten to fifteen feet away from the first player, directly in front of the line. Three small cones are placed in a line, from which the first player in line will start toward the intended target. The distance between the cones depends on the size, age, and skill level of the players. The cones are used to represent the starting or fielding point, the throwing or release point, and the point to which the player should follow the throw after the ball is released.

Using cones as reference points, have the kids catch the ball at Cone #1, make sure they reach Cone #2 when throwing,

The first player in line places his right foot next to the first cone and assumes the ready position. The cone is used as a reference or starting point and should not come into play at all as far as the player attempting to actually field the ball is concerned. It should be to the right of the player's right foot. The coach asks the player to assume a good fielding position and rolls a ground ball toward the open glove. Emphasis should be placed on catching the ground ball correctly. A player can't throw it if he doesn't catch it.

After catching the ball, the player shuffles toward the target, releasing the ball at or near the second cone, and then follows the throw all the way to or past the third cone before returning to the end of the line. After the ball is fielded, it's important to make sure that the player stays low while shuffling his feet. The player should not stand straight up. That's wasted movement, which takes extra time and often disrupts the throwing mechanics. Remind the player to stay low, shuffle, and follow the throw. It's okay to make the player exaggerate the follow portion of this drill for emphasis.

At our camps we like to take this drill a step further and turn it into a contest. At first we have the players throw to a human target, but on the last day we like to have fun with the kids and let them throw toward an inanimate object. We have a cone that's about chest-high that we set right on

and then finish at Cone #3 by following their throw.

second base. The cone has a metal sign on top, and the players field balls as if they're playing third base. We play an elimination game where the kids who hit the sign stay in and those who miss are eliminated. It's a fun way for them to develop the skill that we're trying to teach.

❖ ❖ ❖ ❖ ❖ ❖ ❖ ❖ ❖ ❖ ❖ ❖ ❖ ❖ ❖ ❖ ❖ ❖ ❖ ❖

PERFECT PRACTICE MAKES PERFECT: ROLL THE BALL DRILL

As coaches working with young players in this drill, we want to make the kid catch the ball. We want to develop that feeling of what it's like to be in proper fielding position. This can be as simple as simple gets: We get wide and we get the kids to face the coach, who rolls balls to them. It's a simple thing, but we want to make sure our hands are out in front when we catch the ball, our wrist is in a good position, and our glove is in the right position to receive that ball.

When we do our infield work in the camps, we'll spend three days in the infield with the kids and won't hit one ball. You can't control the hop with a bat, but you can throw them as hard as a kid would get in a game, and have a chance to control the hop. Increase the distance based on the age group. With this drill you're not creating a bad habit by getting bad hops or hitting ground balls on a choppy playing field. For young kids, use a flat surface—gym, tennis court, or artificial turf—to eliminate the fear of bad hops. Success is fun and makes them want to keep playing. Flat surfaces ensure success and build confidence.

◆ ◆ ◆ ◆ ◆ ◆ ◆ ◆ ◆ ◆ ◆ ◆ ◆ ◆ ◆ ◆ ◆ ◆ ◆ ◆

◆ ◆ ◆ ◆ ◆ ◆ ◆ ◆ ◆ ◆ ◆ ◆ ◆ ◆ ◆ ◆ ◆ ◆ ◆ ◆

PERFECT PRACTICE MAKES PERFECT: THROWING-SIDE FOOT BACKHAND DRILL

Have the players line up across from the coach. The player at the front of the line steps to his right with his right leg extended. Then he pivots and goes down on his back knee. What we're doing in this drill is creating a wider base for the backhand play. Bringing the knee down brings the butt closer to the ground and forces the glove hand to be out front. We want the glove hand out in front of that front foot. Our arm is not in play. The coach rolls the ball right at the player's front foot, and he's going to catch it with his hand out front. As coaches in this drill we have to make an accurate roll, because this is a more difficult drill. We have to force the players to catch the ball. This drill is to establish the backhand and where you're supposed to catch the ball: out in front.

* *

* *

PERFECT PRACTICE MAKES PERFECT: GLOVE-SIDE FOOT BACKHAND DRILL

The players start out facing the coach, then they cross over with their left foot. As with the previous drill, they can go down on one knee for comfort. They've established a wide base, rear end low to the ground, hands out in front. This is a lunge-type play and the ball is going to be caught out in front, off the front foot. Young players get hit in the elbow or in the wrist in this drill because they have a tendency to drag their glove behind them. And when you drag the glove behind, it puts your catching arm in the way. So as coaches we make our players catch the ball out in front where they can see it.

* *

* *

BILL'S BALL GAME

The backhand drills are among my favorite drills because the backhand is such an important part of the game. Once you've mastered the backhand drills with your knee down, try raising your knee four to five inches off the ground, to the point where you're getting more upright. For the more advanced player, using the knee for balance isn't necessary, so to take it to the next step, try it standing up.

* *

PERFECT PRACTICE MAKES PERFECT: UNDERHAND TOSS DRILL

Coaches can work on the underhand flip by rolling the ball to each player and having them flip it back and finish by high-fiving the coach. The players should concentrate on catching the ball first and then tossing it with the three fundamentals: momentum toward the target, an accurate flip, and finishing with the hand held up high. Don't let them get into flipper mode or recoil because then they don't have as much control of the toss. Take the ball to the target by using the feet, flip, leave the hand up, and then follow the flip.

The underhand toss drill—in which players high-five the coach after making the toss— is useful for working on the underhand flip.

PERFECT PRACTICE MAKES PERFECT: THE BOX DRILL—SHORT TO SECOND

This box drill is going to simulate the shortstop-to-second-base toss. We make a nice-sized box with four players; the fifth player starts at any corner, and the first toss comes from the corner where there are two players. As you rotate, there's always a player on each corner and one doing the toss. We do this drill without gloves, and when you do it with youngsters you'll see that they don't drop as many barehanded as you might think, because their concentration heightens a little bit.

Facing the corner to your right, you create momentum toward the target to the left by shuffling your feet or crossing over, then flipping the ball low to high and leaving your hand up, following to the next corner. The next person's responsibility is to catch the ball first and then repeat. Keep going all the way around. On an underhand flip, you don't want to have a

loose wrist and you don't want to recoil. If you keep your hand at face level, that's where the ball will end up. There's no need to take the ball behind your back. That's bowling and a wasted motion.

Left and below: *The box drill is another good drill to develop the fundamentals for the underhand flip.*

PERFECT PRACTICE MAKES PERFECT: THE BOX DRILL—SECOND TO SHORT

You can run the same drill to work on the second-base-to-shortstop toss. Here you're facing the corner to your left and creating momentum toward the target to your right. You want to shuffle or cross over; you're not going to square your shoulders to the shortstop. You're going to keep your arm in front of your body. That's where you caught the ground ball to begin with, and that's where the shortstop's eyesight is going to be. So shuffle off, get momentum, hand stays in front, hand stays up.

The most efficient use of your feet, whether shortstop to second base or second base to shortstop, is the crossover step. This movement is slightly more advanced than just shuffling your feet.

FUN FACTOR: PLYWOOD TARGETS

Let your team design and build targets made of plywood. Have fun painting or decorating them. Create little competitions on throwing accuracy at different targets, perhaps even have small rewards for success. Just be certain that everyone can achieve success on some level.

The mind-set here is similar to some of the contests that you may have seen involving an individual who gets a chance to throw a ball through a hole to win a prize. These games teach accuracy. Start out at short distances, but as the accuracy improves, the distance can become greater. The benefit from the greater distances is building arm strength, and the improved accuracy is beneficial to both infield and outfield play.

◆ ◆ ◆ ◆ ◆ ◆ ◆ ◆ ◆ ◆ ◆ ◆ ◆ ◆ ◆ ◆ ◆ ◆ ◆ ◆

◆ ◆ ◆ ◆ ◆ ◆ ◆ ◆ ◆ ◆ ◆ ◆ ◆ ◆ ◆ ◆ ◆ ◆ ◆ ◆

FUN FACTOR: LACROSSE TOSS

Warm up by playing normal catch, slowly increasing the distance. When the players are sufficiently warm, have two goals set up across from each other with half the kids next to each goal and have them try to throw the ball into the other side's net (there's no defending the goal in this game). The ball must have a chance to go into the goal, either on the fly or on the ground. A point system can be established whereby a ball making it in on the fly is worth two points and one making it in on the ground is worth a point. Play to 15.

◆ ◆ ◆ ◆ ◆ ◆ ◆ ◆ ◆ ◆ ◆ ◆ ◆ ◆ ◆ ◆ ◆ ◆ ◆ ◆

FUN FACTOR: JAVELIN TOSS ON FOOTBALL FIELD

Visualize the javelin toss in the Olympics. Now replace the javelin with a baseball. The football field already has distance markers in the form of yard lines. Use the goal line as the line that you have to stay behind when releasing the ball. Have some players or coaches or parents with marking flags act as judges. You could take this concept to whatever fun level you like depending on how you act out the roles of the javelin (baseball) event.

Long-toss is great for building arm strength and to teach throwing the ball with the entire body (not just the arm). Warm up by playing catch while slowly increasing your distance. The warm-up period should take ten minutes, with the final five minutes being long-toss. Use the javelin-style toss as the finisher of your throwing period.

The kids are already warm. Let each player have three throws. Start approximately at the back of the end zone and get a running start for some momentum and release the ball right at the goal line. Instruct the kids to use good form and stay under control. The purpose is not to blow your arm out but to strengthen it. Keep records of the distances for the purpose of self-competition. This event should not be done every day. Once a week, or to breathe some life into a practice, is fine.

FUN FACTOR: LONG-TOSS, GOLF-STYLE

Create a makeshift green with a flag stick in the middle. Create a point system by drawing circles around the flag similar to a dart board. The closer the player's throw lands to the flag, the more points he gets. Walk off a certain distance that's challenging to their arm strength . . . and bombs away. This is not a drill to see how far they can throw. The distance should be long enough to stretch the players out a bit, but still comfortable enough to make 25 to 50 tosses.

◆ ◆ ◆ ◆ ◆ ◆ ◆ ◆ ◆ ◆ ◆ ◆ ◆ ◆ ◆ ◆ ◆ ◆ ◆ ◆

INFIELDER'S CHECKLIST

- Prior to assuming the ready position, the infielders should review the game situation (outs, runners on base, inning, score). Anticipate the ball being hit to you and know what to do if it is.
- As the ball enters the hitting zone, the infielder should assume a ready position: feet spread a comfortable width apart, shoulders square to home plate, weight shifted forward and distributed evenly on the balls of the feet, knees bent slightly, and head up.
- Anticipate that the ball will take a bad hop, and if it does, you'll be ready to field it.
- To field a ground ball, create a wide base with your butt down and your hands out in front.
- Keep your eyes on the ball and see it go into the glove. Try to catch every ball out in front.
- Use two hands whenever possible.
- A crossover step is the first movement side to side. Practice this when the ball comes off the bat in batting practice until it's second nature.

- Work on backhand plays in practice. An infielder can't get in front of every ball, and the ability to backhand is a weapon. The backhand is caught out in front of the body off either foot.
- Know your arm strength as well as the speed of the batter and other runners.
- Always try to know as much about the hitters as you can. Learn from earlier at-bats.
- Be aware of the pitch being thrown and be ready to move one way or the other accordingly.
- In a double play situation, make sure to get the first out. Double plays are rare at the youth levels, so avoiding errors and getting the lead runner should be the focus.
- Middle infielders should perfect the use of the underhand flip. If done properly, the underhand flip can be used to start two-thirds of all double plays.
- When throwing, create momentum to the target, point your front shoulder, and follow the throw.
- Always use a four-seam grip when throwing.
- Remember that balance, rhythm, and timing come with good practice. Practice correctly and you will play correctly.

BEHIND THE PLATE

Handling the Job of Catcher

FIRST THINGS FIRST

By Cal Ripken, Jr.

Dad used to call his catching gear the tools of ignorance. In case you didn't know, Dad was a catcher. He took great pride in the position. To him the catcher was the general on the field. After all, it was the only position that could see all the other positions clearly. It was also the only position that was in foul territory. We can't remember if Dad had a positive comment about that, but knowing him he probably turned that into a positive somehow.

It takes a special kind of player to be a catcher. We both tried it and we both tried to like it because it was Dad's position. Maybe it was all those injury stories that Dad used to relate to us: foul tips off the fingers, a bat through the mask, getting hit with the backswing of a hitter, or just plain getting run over on a play at the plate. Whatever it was, it wasn't right for us.

But a catcher certainly can have a huge impact on the game and the team. The control is right in his fingertips, literally, by calling the pitches. He can be a true on-field manager. He can control the pace of the game. He can be a spark plug and help motivate the team. He's usually the sweatiest and dirtiest guy on the field.

In hockey, kids want to play goalie, and catching has the same draw with young baseball players—kids like the cool equipment they get to wear. Sure, half the battle is getting a kid to *want* to play the position. The other half is to help the young player learn how to deal with the physicality that the position demands, as well as the unselfishness and the fact that in many cases catching will hinder a player's offensive output.

Catchers at a young age should be told up front about the physical pain that often is involved in playing the position. There are also going to be kids who want to bite off more than they can chew, trying things they probably aren't physically and mentally ready for. Always take into account the safety factor. Other kids, who may be backup infielders or outfielders, can catch and don't even know it. Encourage players who have strong arms and display good footwork to try the position.

Catcher is the "tough guy" position. A certain amount of durability is needed. A catcher must want to be a leader on the field. (Every position should be aware of what the other positions' responsibilities are, but with catchers it's a must.) A good catcher can be developed fundamentally, but a certain personality is just as important. If you can't get along with pitchers (which often means dealing with their egos) and umpires, you're in trouble as a catcher. A catcher should be unselfish. Getting the pitching staff to look good and be successful is the bottom line. That will lead to winning.

Dad was all of these things. It would have been nice to see him fulfill his dream of catching in the big leagues, but it wasn't meant to be. He was injured one night when he sustained two hard foul balls off the same spot on his throwing shoulder. It affected his ability to throw, and it took five years for his arm strength to return. Good thing for a lot of Oriole players over the years that Dad went straight into coaching and managing in the minor leagues. It's always been said that the best baseball instructors and managers were once catchers.

That's certainly true of Mark Parent, Ripken Baseball's catching guru, whose expertise was invaluable in the writing of this chapter. Mark played 13 years in the big leagues, and he could certainly swing the bat (he hit 18 homers in 81 games in 1995), but he was also a tremendously skilled and smart defensive catcher. His career fielding percentage is .990, better than that of Hall of Famers Johnny Bench, Yogi Berra, and Carlton Fisk. Mark is a big guy—6'5", 245 pounds—so he was able to withstand the rigors of the catching position. But he was also agile enough to block pitches in the dirt. Beyond all the physical tools, though, he used his head at all times. As a catcher you have to do that.

Well, we've either scared you away from being a catcher or appealed to your desire for the greater sense of control and responsibility that catching provides. If it's the latter, tear into our catching fundamentals. We hope you love it all as much as Dad did.

CATCHER'S GEAR

It starts with an athletic supporter with cup. That's number one because it's the most important. Catchers also need a helmet with the ears covered and mask strapped to it. You don't want to guess if the mask is going to stay on during a pitch. You also want a mask with as large a throat protector as possible. Hockey-type masks are good, but don't forget about the throat area.

The chest protector should cover the groin area with a flap and should cover as much of the throat area as possible. As for shin guards, make sure the kneecap is fully protected in the squat position. Shin guards are always hooked with the hook on the outside of the leg. You don't want to run and have the hooks get tangled and cause you to fall. Shin guards also should cover as much of the toe as possible.

❖ ❖

CAL'S CORNER

Get a catcher's mitt that you're comfortable with. The type and shape of your mitt can hinder or assist you in the time of your mitt-to-hand transfer. And when you're trying to throw out a would-be base stealer, every split second counts.

❖ ❖

SIGNAL STANCE

As a catcher your basic stance, or signal stance, is the one that you start out in before the pitch is thrown. Take your basic athletic position and squat. Once you squat, simply adjust how wide apart your feet are. In this situation, squatting so that you're comfortable is important. You should be in a comfortable, balanced, athletic position, and your knees should be apart but just wide enough so that your signs are visible to the pitcher. You don't want them too far apart because you want to keep the opposing players and coaches from seeing the signs. The hand that you give the signs with should be placed close to your cup. If it's too high or too low, you may give away the signs.

It's important for the catcher to be in a comfortable, balanced position that allows him to hide the signs.

GIVING SIGNS

Giving good signs seems like a small detail. But as we always say in this game: If you don't take care of the little things, you'll have big things to worry about. When it comes to giving signs, little things can cost you stolen bases, runs, and, ultimately, ball games. If your signs are too low, they can and will be relayed from either the dugout or the on-deck circle. If your legs are spread too far apart when you give signs, the runner at first base can see them and may attempt to steal when you call an off-speed pitch. If your glove hand is resting on top of your left leg, the third-base coach can relay the sign to the batter or to the baserunner.

To give signs properly, while in your squat position, place your mitt in front of your left knee to block the view of the third-base coach. Spread your legs apart so that only the pitcher, shortstop, and second baseman can see the signs. If a runner is on first, simply close your leg a bit on that side. Take your forearm and stick it as deep as possible into the hip flexor area and then grab your cup. This will help you make sure the signs are deep enough not to be seen, and not too low as well.

RECEIVING STANCE

Now that you've given the sign and the pitcher is getting ready to throw, you're getting ready to catch the ball. The first important element of your receiving stance is comfort—that's going to enable you to free up your hands more easily to adjust to the pitch and to be ready to throw quickly if necessary.

⊘ You shouldn't have your fingers too low, and your mitt should cover the signs.

You also need to be relaxed so that you can receive the pitch with soft hands and give the umpire the best possible chance to see a strike. To maximize your flexibility, your elbows should be outside your shin guards and your glove-hand wrist should be loose. You should be on your insteps instead of your toes, because that way when you're receiving the ball—whether it's outside, inside, or what have you—you can get weight transfer in any direction. You don't want to be back on your heels; your weight should be out in front.

To get your mitt into the best catching position, make a slight counterclockwise turn with your glove hand. Where you place your throwing hand is a matter of personal preference to some degree, but you should have it somewhere comfortably behind your body. For youth players in this situation, it's important to protect your throwing hand. Many young players put their

When receiving pitches it's important to have your mitt out in front and your throwing hand protected behind your right leg.

hand behind their back, but doing this puts more weight back on your heels. This will make it more difficult to move toward the ball. A better place for your hand is behind your mitt or alongside the outside part of your leg, where it's protected, and your weight is more forward than back. How many people like to do anything with one hand tied behind their back?

With runners on base or two strikes on the hitter, your rear end should be slightly higher and your weight slightly forward, with your throwing hand protected behind your mitt.

RUNNERS ON BASE—TWO STRIKES STANCE

With runners on base or two strikes on the hitter, you should adjust your stance slightly to get into the best possible throwing position. Getting into the proper stance in this situation is essential. Not only are you worried about getting strikes called, but you also have running situations that can occur. And, of course, when a batter has two strikes on him, you need to be able to block a wild pitch. You want to be in a good, athletic position, ready to throw a runner out or block a pitch in the dirt.

The difference is that in this situation you want to keep your rear end up high enough to either throw or block a pitch in the dirt. Both knees should be pointing toward second base. Try to keep the feet just off-line: the right toe in line with the left arch. And stay on the balls of your feet. If your rear end is down and you're flat-footed, your first movement has to be up. You want to be able to go through the pitch to throw and go down and through a pitch to block it. Your throwing hand should be placed behind the catcher's mitt in case of foul balls, and that hand should be balled up loosely into a fist to prevent foul balls off the fingers. Follow the plane of the ball with both hands.

RECEIVING THE PITCH

A catcher should give the pitcher a target that he can see easily. The mitt should be wide open, with the glove hand relaxed. Try to show the target as late as possible, but early enough so your pitcher can have something to focus on. Sometimes when you set up early and give the target too soon, location can be relayed from the on-deck circle or the dugout.

When receiving the ball, think of catching an egg. Try to keep your hands as soft as possible. To accomplish this, you first have to have your body relaxed and, more important, your glove hand relaxed. Being tense makes you slow. In turn, when you feel like you're trying to catch up with the pitch, you snatch at air rather than receiving it.

Try to envision a funnel the size of a strike zone that you want to empty into the center of your body. Catch a pitch into your body, but don't try to receive it too close to your body. The high pitch comes down, the low pitch comes up, and the outer and inner pitches come to the center. Remember to center everything. How you catch the pitch can make the difference between a strike and a ball.

A small alteration in hand placement can be the difference between a strike (left) and a ball ⊘ right).

One of the biggest flaws with most young catchers is that they keep their target too close to their bodies. They end up getting handcuffed. If you have a pitcher who's throwing hard and you have to flinch to catch the ball, that's because you're not out in front enough, and the elbow on your glove arm gets into your knee and you get handcuffed. You want to get your left elbow outside your left knee and get the glove target out in front. If your target is out front, when you receive the ball you have some room to give with it. When pitchers throw hard, sometimes you don't have the reaction time. If your mitt is out in front, you get full movement and have more room to give with the ball. By having your elbow outside the knee, you have all the room in the world. If your mitt is too close to your body, you get locked up.

Try to receive the ball softly, keeping your mitt as loose as you can on your hand. Instead of thinking about catching the ball, let the ball close your mitt: Get your mitt open, loosely on your hand, and let the pitch close it.

◆ ◆ ◆ ◆ ◆ ◆ ◆ ◆ ◆ ◆ ◆ ◆ ◆ ◆ ◆ ◆ ◆ ◆ ◆

BILL'S BALL GAME

When catching the pitch, it's important to remember to follow the ball all the way into your mitt. Don't assume the projection of the pitch, because some pitchers have a lot of late movement and you might get fooled.

◆ ◆ ◆ ◆ ◆ ◆ ◆ ◆ ◆ ◆ ◆ ◆ ◆ ◆ ◆ ◆ ◆ ◆ ◆

BLOCKING BALLS

Blocking balls is often what distinguishes the good catchers from the fair catchers from the great catchers. It shows whether you really love catching. Guys who can block pitches on a regular basis and enjoy doing it are the good catchers. It's probably the toughest thing to do and probably the toughest thing to *enjoy* doing, because often it hurts. This is where you are going to take your lumps. But there's an art to doing it.

To block a pitch you must have flexibility. Always anticipate the ball in the dirt, especially when the hitter has two strikes or when there are runners on base. Your throwing hand should be tucked safely behind your catcher's mitt and the mitt should be placed between your legs to prevent balls from rolling in between your legs. Your butt should be as close to the ground as you can get it and still have flexibility.

Try to create good angles with your body when blocking balls in order to control them better. Swing your hips around to create the angles parallel to the shape of the plate. Try to catch the ball with your chest protector, not your mitt. Keep your chin down in order to prevent the ball from hitting your neck.

When blocking a ball in the dirt, it's important not to give the ball any room to escape.

Turning the hips on balls off the plate makes the ball bounce toward home plate and remain in the catcher's control.

⊘ A common error young catchers make when blocking the ball is staying too upright and turning the head. This gives you less of a chance to make the play and a greater chance to get hurt.

You want to block everything back into fair territory. A lot of times in a game when a ball gets blocked off to the side, the runner advances or scores. So you want to keep the ball in fair territory as much as you can. It's harder to go from right to left. When you kick out to the right, throw your right shoulder. When you kick out to the left, throw your left shoulder. That will promote the position of being able to block everything to the inside.

Many times you'll see a catcher use the backhand and pick the ball out of the dirt with his body out of position. You can always beat yourself up about the way you just blocked a ball, but the bottom line, again, is to get the job done. The point is that you should practice the correct way of blocking a ball time and time again, but in a game it doesn't always work out that way. In a game the bottom line is what counts: keeping that ball in front of you.

Many coaches these days are teaching catchers to kick their feet out to block. We don't like that. The first thing you have to do when kicking your feet out is come up a bit. This is a waste of time, and you don't gain any ground on the pitch by going up first when ultimately the goal is to get down.

When you're in that stance that says, "I'm ready for anything," the first thing you must do is anticipate a ball in the dirt, especially with off-speed pitches and curveballs. When you've got a breaking ball coming in at 80–90 miles per hour, if you want to get to the spot to block it, you must anticipate— beat the pitch to the spot.

What we mean by beat the pitch to the spot is that if you're able to get to where the pitch is going to bounce earlier, you'll have the ability to cut down the height of the bounce, thus minimizing the different angles the ball can bounce off you. This isn't accomplished by kicking your feet out. Since a catcher's stance in this situation is one that has you prepared to throw, receive, and block, you want to be forward and down instead of up and down.

Blocking pitches is a matter of hustle, a relaxed (and confident) frame of mind, and weight distribution. If your weight is back toward your heels with your butt down, you're in trouble. One way that weight is kept back is by having your throwing hand behind you or to the side of your body. That's why we like to see the throwing hand behind the mitt. Four things are accomplished this way: The weight distribution automatically comes forward; it enables you to go through the target to throw to the bases on stolen base attempts; on a stolen base attempt you're able to transfer the ball to your throwing hand as soon as possible; and it enables you to gain ground on wild pitches. You want to get your butt up high so that you can get down to your knees more quickly.

So, with your good stance, anticipation, and weight distribution, you have a chance to go down and through the pitch. Wild pitches to either side should be blocked at a 45-degree angle so the ball ends up somewhere around home plate. Remember, anticipate a breaking ball to a righthanded hitter. You load a bit more of your weight on the left leg so you can get a good push with a 45-degree angle to hold the runners.

If you practice this, the main thing is to tell yourself that you're not catching the ball with your mitt but with the chest protector. You try as hard as you can to smother the ball with your chest. The chest protector is nice and soft, and it's going to provide the best chance to smother the ball and give you a true bounce. Taking the mask to the spot where the pitch bounces puts your head over the baseball and enables you to create a proper angle. Be sure that your throwing hand is behind your target and stays where it is—protected by the mitt, which should be on the dirt between your legs. And it's important to pick up the ball with your bare hand the first time.

THROWING

For a catcher, a big part of throwing is footwork. You should anticipate that every runner is stealing on every pitch. But it's important to catch the ball first—don't try to cheat and get a jump on the throw. Don't reach for the pitch; catch it as deep as possible so that your hands are close to your body and you're in a better position to get the ball out of your mitt and into your throwing hand. Receive the pitch first and make the transfer afterward (your first job is to get a strike call for your pitcher). If you let the pitch get too close to your body, your first movement is to stand up. Throw the ball with a four-seam grip, like any infielder.

When throwing to second base, receive the ball with two hands, transfer it from glove to hand out in front, step through with the right foot, create momentum toward the target, and get the front foot pointed directly at second base. This puts you in a sound throwing position.

You want to get all your momentum going toward the base that you're throwing to. Point your shoulder toward the target. You can't control the pitcher's time to the plate, but you can control the time it takes you to make your throw. You want to do it quickly, but the most important thing is to get balanced; that puts you in the best position to make a strong and accurate throw.

FIELDING BUNTS

The scoreboard and the game situation will dictate how you approach a bunt play. If the opposing team is sacrificing—saying that they'll give up an out to advance a runner—then it's important for a catcher to anticipate the situation and to know these factors: the score, which bases are occupied, the speed of the baserunner(s), and the speed of the batter.

For a catcher, fielding a bunt is much like fielding a ball at any other position. Keep your knees bent—even bunts take bad hops. Pick the ball up with your bare hand so you can pick it up the first time; if you try to use your big, clumsy catcher's mitt you'll usually have to try more than once to pick up the ball. You can use your mitt to assist your bare

When fielding a bunt down the first-base line, it's important to field the ball first, clear yourself from the runner, and make the throw.

hand. Anticipate that you're going to be the one who's going to field the bunt; waiting for the pitcher can often prove costly.

Once you've picked up the ball, keep your feet moving so that you can get your feet and your left shoulder aimed at the target (whichever base you're throwing to). Try to walk through the throw. This will help ensure that you have balance and are aiming your front shoulder toward the target.

On a bunt down the first-base line, once you've fielded the ball you need to clear yourself from throwing it into the runner's path. Take one or two steps toward the infield to give yourself and the first baseman a good line of vision.

CATCHING POP-UPS

Being able to keep your eyes open while the hitter swings at the pitch is crucial. This will help you get a good jump on the ball, and when wearing catcher's gear, this is important. The first thing to do on a pop-up is identify the rotation of the ball. Start out by facing the backstop. Remove your mask quickly and throw it into safe territory once you've determined the flight of the ball. You toss it aside so that you can catch the ball with two hands. If the pop-up is straight up, toss the mask a good distance away to the right. If the pop-up is toward the first-base dugout, throw the mask toward the third-base dugout. In other words, throw the mask in the opposite direction of where you're planning to catch the pop-up. It would be embarrassing to trip over it, let alone to trip over it and not make the play. (If they give you an out, take it!)

Next, you want to keep your feet moving without crossing them. Then, after you're under the ball, get to where the ball would hit you in the nose, and you'll catch it. You should use two hands if at all possible, catching the ball away from your body and above your eyes, allowing you to see the ball and the mitt at the same time. Look the ball into your mitt.

If you're trying to catch the ball up high and you get fooled, then you've got some room to move. It's just like catching a pitch: If you're in tight to begin with and you get handcuffed or fooled, you don't have much room to adjust. But if you're out in front, you have some room to give. Same

thing on a pop-up. You want to get a real good base, with your mitt up above your head.

You don't want to be flat-footed—you want to be on the balls of your feet, with a little flex in your knees so you can be in an athletic position to field the ball. If you end up all the way up against the backstop to make the catch and a runner wants to try to tag up on you, if you're flat-footed when you catch the ball, you have to go from that flat-footed position—not ready—to a throwing position. Whereas if you're on the balls of your feet, you catch the ball and then you just make the glove-to-hand transfer to get back into throwing position.

The catcher should wait until he's certain where a pop fly is going to come down, then discard his mask and make the play.

If you're attempting to catch a pop-up in fair territory in front of home plate, without crossing your feet, you should still get into a position with your back toward the mound. The flight of the ball, because of the backspin, will be a little tricky if you don't do this. But the bottom line is to catch it however you can.

A catcher goes for pop-ups down both baselines and toward the dugout until he is called off. The first and third basemen are coming in and have a much easier play. As a catcher, however, you can't take it for granted that the ball will be caught.

You must be aggressive until called off. Communication is very important: Let people know who has the ball.

RECEIVING THROWS AT THE PLATE

There are two main scenarios that catchers will encounter that involve receiving a throw. The first is when there are fewer than two outs and a runner on third who attempts to score on a ground ball to an infielder.

In this situation, start by getting in position in *front* of home plate so that you're able to see both the runner and the infielder getting ready to make the throw. Get in a good athletic position with your left foot pointed up the third-base line, making sure your knees are bent slightly. If you were going to get rid of the mask, this would be the time, but we suggest leaving it on if possible.

Get your hands out in front as if giving a target to the infielder. Remember, be as relaxed as possible and always anticipate a bad throw to the plate (The situation in the game will determine if you should block a bad throw or try to pick it and make the tag.)

After receiving the throw to the plate, get the ball in your throwing hand inside your mitt as soon as possible (if you have time). This will keep the runner from knocking the ball loose during the play at the plate. Remember to concentrate on *catching the ball first*.

When setting up for the throw at home plate, the catcher should force the runner to slide to the back of home plate. Once he receives the throw the catcher can ride the baserunner further away from the plate.

Once you've received the ball, turn your head as soon as possible to detect the path the runner is taking. Since your left foot is pointing down the baseline, you're giving the runner a path to slide to the back of the plate (at least we hope that's what he'll do). Receive the throw and then push your body down and across the base path by home plate. This pushes the runner away.

If the runner decides not to slide, then do your best to hold on. Remember to stay in an athletic position, more like a linebacker in football. The runner who doesn't slide isn't just trying to score anymore. He's trying to knock you over. So you have to make the tag, but you also have to protect yourself.

The second scenario is when you have a throw coming from the outfield to the plate. Again, get in an athletic position (knees bent, shoulder-width apart, balanced). If the throw comes in the air, the play is the same as receiving a throw from the infield. But when a throw from the outfield comes in on a hop, the catcher becomes an infielder, keeping his mitt low to keep the ball from skipping through. That enables him to come up in case of a bad bounce.

Once you have the ball, all previous tag rules apply. If you have a chance to keep the other team from scoring, you need to do whatever it takes. Catch it first, then make the tag.

While taking infield practice, always take throws from the outfield with your mask on. This allows you to simulate a game situation and is a safer way to receive throws as well. You should also wear a mask when you warm up a pitcher.

◆ ◆

PERFECT PRACTICE MAKES PERFECT: BLOCKING BALLS DRILL

Catchers can work on blocking balls in a separate drill in which a coach throws pitches in the dirt. The throws don't have to be all over the place: The coach should just keep the ball in the dirt, in a relatively small circle in front of the catcher. Take five or ten reps and have the catcher quickly point to where the ball is in the dirt. For young players you can also use spongy balls or tennis balls. The point of the drill is to work on technique: You don't want them to be afraid of getting hit. Graduate to regular baseballs as the catchers gain confidence.

◆ ◆

PERFECT PRACTICE MAKES PERFECT: POP-UP DRILL

Catchers can practice catching pop-ups shot out of a machine. You're not going to catch every one in a perfect position, but you want to work toward that. Concentrate on getting a read on the ball and getting rid of the mask. Get under it and don't just drop the mask—wing it out of there. Go after the ball with two hands. Get your back turned to the outfield. If you're completely square, when you move from side to side you're in a better receiving position. The quicker you can get to the spot and get camped under the ball, the easier it is. If you're going out there half-speed, you're going to drift and your hands aren't going to be in a good position.

FUN FACTOR: RAPID-FIRE PITCHES

A game that can help a catcher develop loose, quick hands is to line up five or six teammates twenty feet in front of home plate. Arm each one with at least six balls. The catcher, in full gear, receives one pitch after the other, right on down the line, in rapid fire. Don't be ridiculous and have everybody throw all at once. The catcher will receive the pitch and let it fall out of his mitt as he relaxes to catch the next pitch.

THE CATCHER'S CHECKLIST

- Durability and anticipation are two important characteristics of a good catcher.
- You should be relaxed and comfortable in your stance, in an athletic position on the insteps of your feet.
- Proper footwork is crucial in all aspects of catching.
- Your target should be out in front and in position to give the umpire the best possible view of the strike zone.

- When receiving the ball, have a relaxed mitt, and roll the mitt a quarter-turn as the pitch is coming. Catch the ball as if it were an egg.
- Funnel any pitch that has the potential to be a strike into the center of your body. But don't try to fool the umpire on pitches that don't have a chance at being called a strike. Catch the low strike up, not by turning the mitt over.
- The most important thing is to receive the pitch first. Then be concerned about getting a strike for the pitcher and trying to throw out the runner.
- Position your throwing hand behind the mitt to start the mitt-to-hand transition of the ball as soon as possible. Find the four seams and get into throwing position as quickly as possible.
- The basic fundamental of pointing your front shoulder and back foot perpendicular to your target is important for throwing and helps keep the ball on the straight and accurate path.
- Anticipation is key for blocking balls in the dirt.
- Get your knees to the proper spot as quickly as possible. Cut down the angles, preferably to a 45-degree angle, and direct wild pitches back toward home plate.
- When blocking a pitch, putting your face over the ball helps cut down the angle of the hop, eliminating a higher bounce that's tougher to control.
- On a pitch in the dirt, pick up the ball with your bare hand the first time. The quicker you can do this, the better chance you have to keep a runner from advancing.
- Pitches that are wild should be blocked however possible, be it backhand or diving—regardless of technique. This is especially important with a runner on third base.
- When fielding a bunt, anticipate that you're the one who's going to field the ball—don't wait for the pitcher or anyone else. Pick up the ball the first time.
- When catching pop-ups, take off your mask as soon as possible and find the ball. While moving in the direction of the ball, discard the mask by tossing it in the opposite direction of the ball landing area, thus eliminating the possibility of tripping over it.

IN THE OUTFIELD

The Last Line of Defense

FIRST THINGS FIRST

By Bill Ripken

Outfielders are probably the most overlooked players on a baseball field. Sure, many of them receive their share of attention from the fans and media. You'll read or hear about the home runs they hit, the runs they drive in, or the bases they steal. Most of what you hear about outfielders is a result of their offensive contributions. Okay, every now and then on *SportsCenter* you'll see someone leaping over a fence to rob a home run. The spectacular defensive play certainly does get recognition. However, the little things that an outfielder does—the things that can save a run here and there, the things that help win ball games over the course of a long season—more often than not are taken for granted.

A quick look at the dictionary illustrates my point. The *Webster's* definition of *outfield* first says, "The part of a baseball field beyond the infield and between the foul lines." That is followed by a second definition: "The baseball defensive positions comprising of right field, center field and left field." Finally, below that is the definition of *outfielder:* "The players who occupy these positions."

Not one of these definitions talks about what an outfielder does or how valuable he can be to a team. As far as most people are concerned, outfielders are guys who occupy the grassy area beyond the infield dirt. They catch a few fly balls every now and then and hopefully contribute some offensive production. Too often the real importance of an outfielder to his team is overlooked. Just as I believe that a good first baseman makes the second baseman, third baseman, and shortstop better, so too does a good defensive outfield make an entire team better.

The number one job of an outfielder is to catch fly balls. If I had to print up a job description of an outfielder, this would go at the top of the list. The second responsibility of an outfielder is to field a ball that's a hit and to throw it back to the infield before the runner can advance to the next base. Beyond that, you would be hard-pressed to get anyone to agree on what should be listed next on an outfielder's job description.

Those first two items certainly are an important part of playing the outfield. There are, however, many other things that an outfielder must do to become a complete defensive player. These are the things that go unnoticed but can really help the ball club.

The simplest way to illustrate the importance of an outfielder in a situation in which he would normally not get credit for helping the team is to look at a typical big league inning:

The leadoff batter steps to home plate and hits a line drive over the second baseman's head toward the right-centerfield gap. The center fielder quickly moves into position to cut off the ball, fields it, spins, and makes a strong, accurate one-hop throw to second base, holding the batter to a single. The next batter steps in and hits a two-hopper to the second baseman, who starts a 4-6-3 double play. Finally, the third batter hits a fly ball to fairly deep left field. The left fielder makes the catch and the inning is over: no runs, one hit, no runners left on base.

Now, let's look at that scenario a little differently, assuming that the outfielder who fielded the first batter's hit didn't do his job:

The first batter hits the ball into the gap and the center fielder either gets there too late or bobbles the ball, allowing the batter to advance to second base. The next batter hits a ground ball to the second baseman, who makes the play to first with the runner from second moving to third. Batter number three hits a fly ball fairly deep to left field, and the runner tags up from third and scores.

All three hitters in the second scenario did the same thing as they did in the first scenario, but the fact that the center fielder didn't do his job on the base hit cost his team a run. At the highest levels of baseball, the outfielders who are willing to work on all of the little things that go into playing the position—the crossover and drop steps, cutting balls off in the gaps, fielding ground balls cleanly, and making strong, accurate throws to the right bases—are the ones who get the job done and who often go unnoticed. In that first scenario, most people would congratulate the second baseman and shortstop for turning the double play or the pitcher for getting out of the jam, when in reality it was the outfielder who held the runner to a single who made the most important play.

During my career I had the opportunity to play with many different outfielders. I played with guys who had great arms and guys who had tremendous foot speed. But out of everyone I played with, Joe Orsulak was probably the most complete outfielder, because he worked at it so hard. Joe had a strong, accurate arm and good foot speed. But he worked every day on all the little things to make himself into a complete outfielder. He realized that if a ball wasn't hit to him he still had a responsibility to the team to back up an infielder, an outfielder, or a throw. When Cal and I discussed assembling a core staff of instructors to work at our camps and clinics, Joe was one of the first names that popped into our minds.

In 1991 Joe had one of the greatest defensive years of any outfielder I've ever seen. He made just one error in 299 chances. Even more impressive, though, was his major-league-leading 22 assists from the outfield. Joe didn't get all of those assists on his own. If there was a runner on first and a ball was hit to the wall in right-centerfield with Joe playing right field, he knew immediately that there was going to be a chance for a play at third base or home. He also knew that he wasn't going to be able to pick the ball up and throw it all the way to third or home. Joe was smart enough to know that he needed my help, just like I knew I needed his. He knew that if he picked up the ball and made a strong, accurate throw that I could handle, I would have a chance to make the relay and get an out at either third or home.

Joe understood his responsibility and knew that if he executed it properly, his job was done and I had a chance to do the rest. He did a lot of things well on the baseball field (Joe played 14 seasons in the big leagues and compiled a .273 career batting average), but he still worked hard every day to improve.

Another former teammate who has been a part of our core instructional staff is Kenny Gerhart. Kenny is not as well known as Joe, having played with Cal and me for parts of three seasons in Baltimore, but he also knew the areas in which he needed work and was smart enough to figure out ways to compensate for his deficiencies. Kenny possessed great foot speed, but didn't have as strong an arm as some big league outfielders. He would use his speed and quickness to make up for his arm. Kenny was as good at going after a ball—in the air or on the ground—as anyone I've ever seen. He would get to balls so quickly and cut them off that his arm wouldn't be a factor. Kenny would have the ball in his control before a runner had the opportunity to decide to go to the next base.

Joe and Kenny have been involved in our camps and clinics since 1999. They've allowed us to build on the base of knowledge that Cal and I have assembled, and the fact that they both played for Dad—and that he appreciated their approach to the game—gives us great comfort when they're teaching young players how to play the outfield the Ripken Way. Their influence can be found throughout this chapter.

As long as a young player understands that there's a lot more to being a good outfielder than occupying that grassy area between the foul lines, and that there are a lot of little things that can always be improved upon to contribute to the success of the team, the rest will take care of itself.

THE READY POSITION

Before the ball is delivered, the outfielder should assume an athletic, ready position: weight distributed evenly on the balls of the feet, knees bent, and legs a comfortable width apart, creating a solid, balanced foundation. Stay relaxed but ready. If you're tight, you react slowly. Don't be flat-footed. Be able to move quickly, always anticipate that the ball's

Just as in the infield, the outfielder's ready position should be an athletic one.

going to be hit to you, and know what you're going to do when that happens. Set up with your shoulders square to the hitting zone and focus your vision there as the ball approaches home plate.

You can put your hands on your knees until the ball's going to be delivered, but then the hands have to come off. The reason for this is that if you have your hands on your knees and the ball's hit to you, what's the first movement that you have to make? You have to take your hands off your knees. That's one movement that we want to eliminate, because every excess movement in the outfield can cost you.

It's imperative for an outfielder to always pay attention. Outfielders should know the situation in the game (number of outs, score, location of runners, type of hitter at the plate) and make sure that their undivided attention is focused on the hitting zone as the ball approaches home plate. Murphy's Law applies: As soon as an outfielder's attention drifts, the ball is sure to find him. A big league center fielder makes about 2.1 putouts per game. At that rate, a 50 percent success rate isn't very good, so paying attention is key.

◆ ◆ ◆ ◆ ◆ ◆ ◆ ◆ ◆ ◆ ◆ ◆ ◆ ◆ ◆ ◆ ◆ ◆ ◆ ◆

BILL'S BALL GAME

One thing we teach young outfielders is that they must be square to home plate. There's no sense in setting up at an angle as a starting point. You want to be square to home plate so you can go in either direction equally well. Once you start playing and figure out that maybe you're a little weaker going one way, you might cheat a little bit with your feet. But a good starting point is to be square to home plate. That's going to give you the best chance to make the play.

◆ ◆ ◆ ◆ ◆ ◆ ◆ ◆ ◆ ◆ ◆ ◆ ◆ ◆ ◆ ◆ ◆ ◆ ◆ ◆

STRAIGHTAWAY POSITIONING

All outfielders—all fielders, for that matter—must understand the concept of straightaway positioning. For an outfielder, the best way to determine straightaway positioning is to reference the bases. By drawing an imaginary line from first base through second base and into left field, the left fielder can determine where straightaway left actually is. The right fielder can do the same by drawing an imaginary line from third base through second base and into the outfield. The center fielder can simply use second base and home plate in a similar fashion. Of course, the actual depth that determines where straightaway is varies from age group to age group.

Outfielders will shift their positioning throughout the game depending on the situation, the pitcher, and the batter. For example, when playing on the road with fewer than two outs and the winning run on third, outfielders should play short enough to provide a good shot at the man trying to score. This also might enable the outfielder to handle a line drive that would otherwise fall for a base hit. But, especially at the younger ages, an outfielder who plays too close to the line or too close to another fielder can create a huge advantage for opposing hitters. This also can be dangerous if the outfielders have not learned to communicate properly. Adjustments sometimes need to be made off the straightaway position. The outfielder must have clear vision to home plate to get his jump. Sometimes an infielder or pitcher will block the outfielder's view. In this case, he needs to adjust two or three steps to regain his view.

❖ ❖

CAL'S CORNER

Some fields can be disorienting, so the bases are always the most consistent point of reference that you can use. If you go into Fenway Park and the Green Monster's right there behind you, it might seem like you're not playing in the right position. But the bases are still the same distance apart: 90 feet. So from left field you can look right down the line from second to first base and use that as your point of reference to determine where the straightaway position is. I used to do the same thing at shortstop. Yankee Stadium is cut out really big, so I would stand out in the middle and dissect the line between second and third and look right to home plate. And sometimes in early practice I'd come out and mark it because it would seem to change a bit when the field got played on or when it got to be nighttime.

❖ ❖

AS THE PITCHER DELIVERS

There are two methods of picking up the baseball after it's delivered by the pitcher. Whichever method is used should be determined by an individual player's comfort level. The first is to focus on a spot in front of home plate as the ball leaves the pitcher's hand. (Younger players should try to focus on the general hitting zone; with experience outfielders will learn where certain hitters tend to make contact and can focus on that area.) This is easier for some players, who find it difficult to follow the ball all the way from the pitcher's hand to the hitting zone and then back out to the field when the ball is hit.

The second method is to watch the ball all the way from the pitcher's release point to the point of contact. This method is more difficult for a lot of players (the outfielder's head usually whips back and forth from the release point to the point of contact, causing the outfielder to take an extra split second to judge the flight of the ball). But again, each player should determine which method is most comfortable. Square your body to the hitting zone as the pitch is delivered. This will allow you to break either left or right after the ball comes off the bat. And if you angle and the ball is hit over the opposite shoulder, you lose two steps trying to square your body and then cross over to go after the ball. In either case, the head needs to be still when the pitch reaches the zone. This allows the eyes to pick up the batted ball more quickly.

GETTING TO THE SPOT

As an outfielder you want to try to get to the spot where the ball is going to come down as fast as you can. You're not going to time it so that the ball's coming down and you're getting to the spot. You're going to try to get to the spot before the ball comes down. This takes a little practice at the younger levels, but the young players are going to get the idea. The idea is if you get to your spot before the ball comes down and you misjudge it you have time to make an adjustment—to go back, forward, right, or left. If you're cruising on the ball and the wind catches it or you misjudge it, the ball drops because you have no time to recover.

From the ready position, the outfielder uses a quick crossover step in moving to his left or right. This enables him to get to the ball as quickly as possible so that he can make the play with a good throw. At this time he should know what he's going to do with the ball and where he's going to make his throw.

There are no automatic first moves for an outfielder. The first move is determined by where and how the ball is hit. A coach should resist telling an outfielder to take an automatic step back to compensate for a ball over his head; instead, teach the proper fundamentals and work on weaknesses.

◆ ◆

BILL'S BALL GAME

Conditioning is important for outfielders. You should run lots of sprints and work on long strides. The outfielder should be in the best condition on the team. You have to cover longer distances, even backing up plays, so you can never afford to have tired legs out there.

◆ ◆

By catching the ball above the head the outfielder has the best chance of success.

CATCHING A FLY BALL

The number one job of any outfielder is to catch the fly ball and record the out. It doesn't matter if an outfielder catches the ball on the right side, the left side, or the center of his body, as long as the glove and the other hand are above the eyes. The most important thing is to be able to see the ball *and* the glove.

We teach younger players to catch fly balls with two hands, provided that they get to the spot, they have time, and there's nobody tagging up. As players become more advanced we like them to catch the ball in the manner that's most comfortable—one hand or two—as long as they can see the ball and the glove.

We teach outfielders to get to the spot where the ball is going to come down and catch it above their head. Catching the ball on the right side

(or throwing side) doesn't necessarily make it easier to get rid of the ball quickly. You still have to bring the ball to the center of your body and separate your hands to throw. Sometimes catching the ball on the throwing side causes a player to throw off the wrong foot, thus rushing his delivery, which can cause a weak or errant throw.

If you have to run and catch the ball, catch it with one hand. You don't want to try to get a ball on the run with two hands because you'll risk tying yourself up. Get to the spot, see the ball, see the glove.

On tag plays the outfielder must try to get to a spot ten feet or so behind where the ball comes down, so he can gain momentum into the ball to make a stronger throw (if time permits).

⊘ Letting the ball travel below your eyesight (left) decreases your chances of catching the ball, and you may get hit in the head!

Even when using one hand on the run, the most important thing is to have the glove above your eyes.

We were teammates on the Orioles for seven seasons and still work together teaching the game.

The key thing to remember when gripping the bat is to hold it loosely in the fingers and line up your "door-knocking knuckles."

Your stride should be short and soft, with the front foot and lead shoulder going toward the pitcher. A proper stride

When bunting, keep the barrel of the bat above your hands and the bat out in front of home plate.

helps create a fast, fluid swing.

We use the tee drill to stress the weight shift, and we tell the hitters to swing with a purpose.

The soft-toss drill is great for developing quick hands; it's important for the feeder to toss strikes.

In the one-arm drill the hitter should take the lead hand on a direct path to the baseball.

When running through first base, you should touch the front part of the bag closest to home plate.

When rounding first base, touch the base in the center of the edge closest to second base, so you can push off.

When taking a lead off first base, keep your eyes on the pitcher and don't cross your feet, so you can get back to the base quickly.

Pitching mechanics can be broken down into five sections. We call them the *Five Links of the Chain*. The **first link** is footwork. That's what the starting position is all about. **A:** *Start with your heel on the rubber and your toes in contact with the ground.* **B:** *A small first step back allows the head to stay over the pivot foot.* **C:** *Make sure your pivot foot makes a full pivot parallel with the rubber.* **D:** *Bring your upper and lower body together to form the* **second** *link, the balance position.*

E: *When going from the balance position to the* **third link**, *the power position, the pitcher must take the baseball down, out, and up from his glove with his hand on top of the ball* (**F**).

Arm action is created when the hand goes from above the ball to behind the ball when throwing (**G and H**).

I: *During the* **fourth link**, *rotation, it's important to keep the elbow above the shoulder, creating an L.* **J:** *When the pitcher releases the ball, both feet should be on the ground.*

K: *If the four prior links are done correctly, the* **fifth link**, *the follow-through, will take care of itself.*

With the four-seam fastball grip, the fingertips should have contact with the seams and the thumb should be under the ball.

On the two-seam fastball, the fingers should also be in contact with the seams.

A lot of people think that with the change-up grip the ball needs to be back in the hand. But it's still thrown with the fingers.

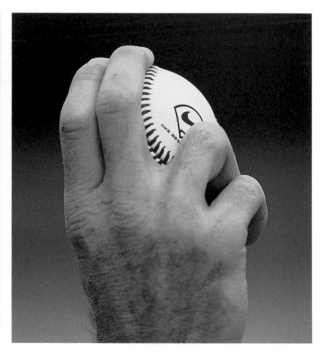

When throwing a breaking ball, it's important for your middle finger to be able to find and use a long seam.

The coach can hold a glove out in front of the pitcher to help him work on his extension. Remember that with a breaking ball you don't have as much extension as with a fastball.

On a pickoff throw, break from the rubber first, then set your feet and make an accurate throw.

The one-knee drill is used to help a pitcher get his hand on top of the ball after taking the ball out of his glove.

When fielding a ground ball you should have a wide base, butt down, and hands out in front.

After catching a ground ball you should generate momentum toward your target and follow your throw.

The crossover step is the most efficient step in baseball.

It's important for the first baseman to get to the bag early and be a good target, square to the infielder who's throwing him the ball. The first baseman's glove and glove-side foot should work in tandem.

The underhand flip can be a valuable weapon for starting double plays at the highest level. An important part of the flip is to show the ball.

The high-five drill—in which players high-five the coach after making the toss—is useful for working on the underhand flip.

The box drill is another good drill to develop the fundamentals for the underhand flip.

Top left and right: *The catcher should be in a comfortable, balanced position that allows him to hide the signs.*

Far left: *When receiving pitches, it's important for the catcher to have his mitt out in front and his throwing hand protected behind his leg.*

Near left: *When blocking a ball in the dirt, a catcher should try to smother the ball.*

Far left: *When throwing to second base, receive the ball with two hands, transfer the ball from mitt to hand out in front, step through with the right foot, create momentum toward the target, and get the front foot pointed directly at second base.*

Near left: *The catcher should wait until he's certain where a pop fly is going to come down, then discard his mask and make the play.*

By catching the ball above his head, an outfielder gives himself the best chance of success. Even when using one hand on the run, the most important thing is to have the glove above your eyes.

After catching the ball, explode toward your target by using your feet, while the rest of your body gets into a good throwing position. Throwing from over the top is recommended, especially from the outfield.

We believe it's important to stress the fundamentals, but just as important to keep things simple and have fun.

BILL'S BALL GAME

How an individual player catches a fly ball is important. I caught fly balls in the infield with one hand on the left side of my body because, for me, if I took my right hand and put it up there, I blocked my vision. And the two eyes in our head are very, very important. If I can see the ball go into my glove, that's what I want. Cal caught almost every infield fly ball with two hands directly above his head where he could see it. I couldn't do that, because that right hand blocked my vision.

Joe Orsulak was one of the best outfielders that I played with; in my opinion there was no one who played better, fundamentally sound outfield defense than Joe. And Joe was a one-handed outfielder. When we talk to young players, we stress using two hands because it's a safeguard. If the ball bubbles out of your glove, your hand is there to help you catch it. But if you see a little kid reach up with two hands and drop the ball, and then later he reaches up with one hand and catches it, I'd have to go with the one-handed approach because that's the one he actually did right.

ROUTINE FLY BALL

A routine fly ball is a ball that's hit where you have plenty of time and there's no one on base. Get your glove up over your head, not down by your chest. We like to say, "Keep your glove between the ball and your eyes." Ball, glove, eyes. If you have your glove above your head between the ball and your eyes, you have to look through your glove to see the ball. Therefore, you're going to follow the ball all the way into your glove. You want to see the ball into your glove. If you have your glove down low, you have to move your head really quickly to keep your eye on the ball. No one can move his head that quickly and keep his eye on the ball, so you'd lose the ball somewhere.

Catch the ball with two hands, with the glove above your head. If you have the glove above your head and you drop the ball, your coach probably isn't going to even say anything to you because you did it the right way. We're all human, and we all miss some. But if you have your glove in the wrong position or you try to catch it one-handed and drop it, your coach is almost certainly going to say something to you about it.

FIELDING A GROUND BALL

Once a batter gets a base hit, it becomes the outfielder's job to keep the batter at first base. The outfielder should get to the spot where the ball is going as quickly as possible and then get under control. Once at the spot, establish a wide base, with the butt down and the hands out in front. Just as in catching a fly ball, it's important for the eyes to be able to see the ball and the glove. Stay low out of your stance, instead of running upright. This will allow you to cover ground more quickly. The ball should be fielded out in front of the front

There are times when the outfielder needs to field a ground ball with one hand. When doing this it's important to have the glove hand out in front with the glove-side foot.

toe. If a quick throw is necessary, the outfielder should use one hand to field the ball. In situations when it's not necessary to throw out the runner, the outfielder may want to field with two hands and may even get down on one knee to keep the ball in front. Once the ball is fielded, the outfielder throws the ball to the proper teammate (base, cutoff, or relay). At that point the outfielder's job is done. Even on routine ground balls, get the ball in quickly to the infielder. Challenging a fast runner can be a mistake that's unnecessary.

FIELDING A GROUND BALL AND THROWING: FAST, SLOW, FAST

If you want to catch and throw on a ground ball, it's a little different. The ball's hit and you bust in. You still want to get low and you still want to get wide, but not by facing home plate. You want to get wide by stepping toward home plate with your glove-side leg forward and your glove outstretched. This way you can get your butt down and catch it out front. You go fast to field the ball, you slow down to make sure you catch it, and then you quickly get into throwing position with your momentum going toward your target. This way, you cut down the distance, you make sure you catch the ball, and you get rid of it quickly—as opposed to going really fast and booting it and having no play. And by playing the ball off your front toe, you ensure that if the ball takes a bad hop it will hit you in the body and stay in front of you.

You're going to make sure you catch it, but you're not going to go slow the whole way. Fast-slow-fast. That's a good terminology for kids to understand: Get to the spot fast. Get yourself under control. Catch the ball. Then go fast again to make a good throw back into the infield. If the hitter gets a single, he earned first base because he got that base hit. But let's not give him second base. And the way you risk that is by coming through too aggressively, too fast, and botching the play. Field the ball, bring it to the center of your body, generate momentum toward the target, and make a strong, accurate throw to the cutoff man. If you bobble the ball, pick it up with your bare hand the first time.

THE CROSSOVER STEP

On balls hit to the outfielder's left or right, efficiency of motion is important. The best way to achieve this is by using a crossover step (see the infield chapter). On a ball hit to the outfielder's right (no matter if the outfielder is lefthanded or righthanded), pivot and take the left foot and cross over in the direction of the baseball. Reverse it for a ball to the left. There should be no wasted motion; try not to bounce as you go after the ball. The crossover step should be the first movement after the ball is hit. This movement needs to be practiced over and over until it becomes second nature. This can be accomplished by breaking on balls during batting practice or by tossing balls to a player's left or right until the movement is mastered.

Your job as an outfielder is to get to the ball as quickly as possible, which means you need to cover the most ground in the least amount of time. What you see a lot is an outfielder with his hands on his knees, and the ball's hit to him—say it's hit to his right. First he takes his hands off his knees. That's one. Then he picks up his right foot and puts it down. That's two. Then he takes his crossover step. That's three. All this time the ball is traveling.

But if you start in the ready position with your hands off your knees and your first move when the ball's hit is the crossover step, you've eliminated those first two wasted motions, which will give you two more steps in the same amount of time. That's going to make a difference between catching the ball and not catching the ball on a lot of occasions. Even in the big leagues you'll see an outfielder run like heck and reach out and the ball just misses his glove. And people say, "What a great try." But sometimes that guy's just not ready. If he had been ready and he had done the proper steps, he'd have caught that ball.

THE DROP STEP

To achieve efficiency of motion on balls hit over the outfielder's head, a drop step should be used. The drop step is a

ball hit to the right side and deep, the first movement should be made with the outfielder's right foot (drop step).

diagonal step back for when a ball is hit deep to either side of the outfielder. It's followed by a crossover step toward the spot where the ball is going to come down. The toughest play for an outfielder to make is when the ball is hit directly over his head. An outfielder should turn to his strong side on this ball, whether it's his right or left.

Just as with the crossover step, the drop step should be practiced until it becomes second nature. And just as with the crossover step, you're covering ground with every move you make. That's what it's all about in the outfield: covering ground in a hurry. If you can't do that, you can't play the outfield. And with both of these moves, the crossover step and the drop step, you're recognizing the ball first. You're not going to guess that the ball is going to be hit over your head, and then the guy hits one in front of you and you can't catch it. You're seeing the ball off the bat and then making your move.

Backpedaling is an advanced skill worth learning in the higher leagues, for instance, in dome stadiums where taking your eye off the ball causes you to lose it. Or a quick backpedal on a ball misjudged over your head, after you've already gotten to the spot. But generally, backpedaling should be avoided. The outfielder should get to the spot where the ball is going to come down as quickly as possible, catching the ball with the glove above the head if possible. Outfielders should avoid drifting or trying to time the catch.

You can't get under every fly ball that's hit to you. There will be instances when you have to make plays on the run. But the goal is to always hustle and make all plays look routine.

OVER-THE-SHOULDER CATCH

Having your head on a swivel allows you to track the fly ball while still running hard.

On a deep ball you'll sometimes have to make an over-the-shoulder catch. Run toward the spot where you think the ball's going to land and then peek over your front shoulder to pick it up. Take a direct route to the spot where you think the ball's going to land.

You really want to get after the ball and you know you have to run hard, but you have to keep your head still. Run on the balls of your feet and run under control. Use the lower half of your body to run, but the upper half of your body has to guide you toward the ball. It's important not to bounce and to keep your eyes steady. That's how you see the ball. If, because of wind or a slight misjudgment, the ball is over the other shoulder, a quick turn of the head will put you back on the ball. Avoid laying the head back while chasing these balls; that tends to disorient you or throw you off-balance.

THROWING FROM THE OUTFIELD

All outfielders should throw over the top using a four-seam grip. Once the ball is fielded, the outfielder should pick a spot on the target's body to focus on. Ideally this spot should be the chest or head. Throwing over the top (as opposed to sidearm) with a four-seam grip allows for maximum carry and reduces the chances of the ball tailing away from the intended target. The rotation generated by a four-seam grip also allows for a truer skip when the outfielder makes a one-hop throw to a base.

The grip is important in the outfield because you have to make longer throws. If you throw the ball with the proper four-seam grip, it's going to create the correct underspin and it's going to go straight as long as you throw it over the top. It's also going to carry further. In the infield you can get away with throwing on an angle because it's a shorter distance. But in the outfield you won't get away with it. If you hold the ball at an angle with a four-seam grip, it's going to tail all over the place and it's going to be difficult for your infielders to catch the throw on relays and cutoffs. So the first thing coaches should teach a young outfielder is how to grip the ball.

If you're preparing to make a throw after the catch, you should catch the ball with your glove side foot forward and your glove out in front, so you can set up to make the throw. Then take a crow hop, or a step-through, and throw it to your target. When you throw a ball, you don't throw only with your arm. You throw the ball with your body.

When you're going to make a throw, you have to look at what you're throwing at. If you come up firing too quickly, all you're going to see is a blur. You may know that the cutoff man is standing out there, but if you just see his body and you let it fly and you're five feet off this way or that way, it can be costly. You have to concentrate on the target. When you come up firing, look at the chest of the player you're throwing to; that's where you're going to hit him. If you aim for that spot, you're not going to hit him on the dot every time, but you'll

After catching the ball in the proper manner it's important to explode toward your target by using your feet, while the

likely miss by a foot or two from 200 feet away, so he can adjust and catch the ball in great shape to make his throw. If your arm isn't as strong, you might aim for his head. If your arm feels pretty strong that day, you may aim for his belt. The point is that you're going to put it in that vicinity because you're aiming at something. It's important to note that an outfielder's job is to make strong, accurate throws to the proper infielder and not to throw runners out. Throwing runners out is the by-product of proper execution. The only exception is a game-ending play.

rest of your body gets into a good throwing position.

CAL'S CORNER

When you throw over the top, the way the ball rolls and cuts through the air is consistent—it has backspin, and that helps it carry. When I go to camps with younger players and try to stress the importance of throwing overhand, they turn it right back on me and say, "Well, you threw it sidearmed." And I say, "Sidearmed is an advanced way to use your arm after you develop your arm." If you want a good, strong, powerful arm, you first have to learn how to develop your arm and throw over the top. After you've mastered that, and as the game gets harder and more advanced, you're going to learn how to throw from different angles and that'll help you play your position better. And I got away with it because I was an infielder.

CAL'S CORNER

A crow hop is a nice way to introduce the younger kids to the first mechanics of throwing. The way I demonstrate it is by lining up the kids in a football field or a gym, depending on the age group, and have them show me how far they can throw the ball. So you evaluate them first—the point being that if you see how they throw first, you'll realize that most kids will try to throw using only their arm as opposed to their whole body. In the early stages, I just let them throw, and then I mark the spot where they threw and say, "This is your world record. You just threw it this far." And you might have a football field where you can actually measure the yards, or you might just throw a tape measure out and have fun with it that way.

I like the term crow hop because it sounds funny and the kids laugh, but the crow hop is how they learn to create momentum toward the target, using their bodies to throw the ball with their arms. So I'll say, "Here's a crow hop." And I'll overexaggerate, but I'll come up and catch it and I'll run up to the line and I'll throw the ball out of sight. I'll lose that ball. I'll invest in a baseball just to make a point. Throw it all the way out there where you can't find it. If you're next to the woods, throw it into the woods. And they'll laugh about it. Then you point to the spot where their throw landed earlier and say, "This is your world record. Let's see you do the crow hop and let's see how far you throw now." Invariably, every single one of those kids, with very few exceptions, will throw the ball farther than they had just thrown before.

◆ ◆

COMMUNICATION

The center fielder is the general in the outfield and should catch any ball that he can reach. Naturally, if the catch would be an easy one for the off-outfielder (left fielder or right fielder), the center fielder should encourage the off-outfielder to make the play. Outfielders should constantly talk to one another. The center fielder should continue to call for a ball after he has called for it the first time, since the call may have come at the same time as the off-outfielder's call, and the players may not have heard each other. The center fielder should alert the right fielder and infielder on his positioning adjustment so there's proper spacing.

You have to talk to one another in the outfield. If no one says anything, the ball drops and the man's on second base. He should've been out, but instead he's standing on second. One play like that can cost you the game. The center fielder has control, but if he doesn't call for the ball and the left fielder or right fielder can get there, one of them should call for it. Somebody should be calling for the ball every time it's hit in the air. Don't just whisper, "I got it," one time. Yell, "I got it, I got it, I got it," so that there's no confusion. Also, if no one calls for the ball and both outfielders are running full speed, they're going to run into each other, the ball's going to drop, and worse, someone could get hurt. The call should be made after the ball reaches its apex, or starts down. Calling balls on the way up often causes misjudgments and dropped balls, because the other fielder has given up on the ball (especially in windy conditions). The left fielder and right fielder must yield to the center fielder.

STUDYING FIELD CONDITIONS

In the big leagues, with all the new ballparks, there are lots of quirks—angled fences, flagpoles, hills on the fields, short fences, high fences, scoreboard fences. Outfielders have to be aware of all these things. Playing on recreational fields like young players do can be even more of an adventure. There can be smooth grass, rough patches, holes, gullies, hard ground, soft ground, and so forth.

When you go to a field for the first time in a while, during batting practice it's important to get out and walk around and see everything. If it's a sunny day, where is the sun? If the right fielder or left fielder has a bad sun field, the center fielder may have to work harder to help him out. What is the field like? Grass or turf? Short grass or deep grass? Smooth or rough? Where are the fences, how tall are they, and are there any holes or weird angles? How wide is the warning track?

In batting practice, take ten or fifteen minutes and act like it's a real game situation and react to the ball off the bat. Get your jump just like it's in a game, even if the ball isn't hit to you. Practice the crossover step to get moving in the direction the ball is hit, even if it's far away from you. Have a coach hit fungoes right at you, to your right, to your left, into the corners, into the sun (use your glove to shield your eyes). Batting practice isn't just batting practice, it's all-around baseball practice. See how the ball comes off the wall. Check the length of the warning track and how hard the wall is. Does it give or is it like a rock?

◆ ◆

PERFECT PRACTICE MAKES PERFECT: FLY BALL COMMUNICATION DRILLS

A simple way to work on catching the ball and communicating in the outfield is to have a coach hit fly balls, or to fire them out of a machine. The machine spits fly balls out a little differently than the ball comes off a bat, but that still can be a valuable way to work on communicating. Young players shouldn't get discouraged if they're having trouble catching the ball off the machine at first. It takes practice. Coaches should stress getting a good jump from an athletic stance, and proper footwork. Outfielders should know their own strengths and weaknesses. Work harder on your weaknesses, but don't avoid working on your strengths.

To work on communication, have the outfielders form two lines, a good distance apart, and have the machine shoot balls in between the lines (you can use Lite-Flites or regular balls, depending on the players' skill level). Then the outfielders communicate and the ball is caught. Have the outfielder make a strong, accurate throw to a cutoff man (which can be another player who rotates out or a coach).

◆ ◆

PERFECT PRACTICE MAKES PERFECT:
THE DROP STEP DRILL

Footwork is important in the outfield, so it's a good thing to work on in practice. In the drop step drill, the players line up and take turns getting into a ready position in front of a coach. When the coach says, "Go!," the player performs the drop step as the coach throws the ball directly over the player's head. Coaches can paint a guide on the field to help the players understand the proper footwork. Coaches can also hit fly balls and ground balls to the side to allow outfielders to work on the crossover step.

PERFECT PRACTICE MAKES PERFECT: LONG-TOSS

Long-toss is the most important drill in building up arm strength and stretching out the arm. Start close and work your way out to a tough distance to reach. Then work your way back in and finish with some strong bullets, concentrating on accuracy. One or two years of this will show vast improvement in arm strength.

PERFECT PRACTICE MAKES PERFECT: THE OVER-THE-SHOULDER DRILL

The over-the-shoulder drill simulates when an outfielder has to turn and go and doesn't have time to look at the ball the whole time. You have to turn and take off like a sprinter, arms to your sides, head down. After about five or six steps, peek back over your shoulder and find the ball. You don't turn your whole body. That's when you get your feet tangled up and fall down. You don't want to run with your arm and glove up and out in front. That slows you down. It's just like a sprinter: You have your head down and are running all out.

Each player gets a ball and takes turns flipping it to the coach, and then taking off running like a wide receiver on a streak pattern. The outfielders work on peeking back over their shoulders and catching the fly ball that the coach throws them (leading them so they can make a running catch).

◆ ◆

PERFECT PRACTICE MAKES PERFECT: THE FENCE DRILL

Coaches should also work with outfielders to get comfortable with going back on a deep ball near the outfield fence. In the fence drill, the outfielders line up and, one at a time, when the coach yells, "Go!," they approach the fence and feel for it with their bare hand as the coach tosses the ball in the air toward the fence.

◆ ◆

◆ ◆

FUN FACTOR: OUTFIELD CONTESTS

Coaches can turn routine fly ball and over-the-shoulder catch drills into elimination contests to make things more interesting for young players. To stay alive in the game the outfielder has to catch the ball cleanly. The coach can also divide the players into two teams and consider using Lite-Flite balls or no gloves, depending on the players' skill level.

◆ ◆

THE OUTFIELDER'S CHECKLIST

- Check playing field conditions and continuously keep tabs on wind and sun conditions. Keep in mind the condition of the outfield surface and the distance to all the fences.
- Know the game situation at all times, such as number of outs, tying and winning runs, and so on.
- Know the opposing hitters and how the pitcher will attempt to pitch to them.
- Watch all the actions of the hitter closely, such as a stance change for hitting to the opposite field, a stance for bunting, a shortening or lengthening of the grip on the bat, or any change that might indicate the direction he's attempting to hit the ball.

- Anticipate that every ball is going to be hit to you. Think, "What am I going to do with the ball when it's hit to my right, my left, in front, over my head, hard, soft?," and so on.
- Take a slightly squat position with your weight off your heels and lean forward when the pitcher releases the ball.
- Move quickly and alertly to and from your position.
- Run on the balls of your feet and make a smooth approach to the ball.
- Back up other outfielders and all throws to bases.
- Back up infielders on balls hit to them.
- Be sure to know where to throw the ball before getting to it.
- Attempt to hit all cutoff men with a chest-high throw.
- Don't make unnecessary throws on which another runner could advance.
- Charge all ground balls with reasonable timing; don't lay back on them.
- Pick the ball up the first time. Use two hands so you don't bobble or drop the ball. Each time you fail to pick up the ball the runner can advance another base.
- Never be caught without sunglasses. One fly ball lost in the sun may cost the game. If sunglasses aren't available, be aware of the sun location and use the glove or off hand as a shield.
- Call plays whenever a call is necessary.
- The center fielder has priority on fly balls. If the center fielder can get to the ball, he should call off the other outfielder repeatedly so there's no confusion.
- Call for the ball loudly, distinctly, and confidently on all fly balls, and take all fly balls that you can handle that are near the infield. Never pressure an infielder by forcing him to make a tough play. The infielder should be going back until the outfielder calls him off.
- Learn how to play fences. On balls that stop at the bottom of a fence, outfielders should make sure they look at the ball when they pick it up, so that they don't have to reach for it more than once.
- Practice taking balls off the bat during batting practice. Much more can be learned by fielding balls off the bat than by any other method. Work on speed and arm strength.

PERFECT PRACTICE MAKES PERFECT

Running a Practice

FIRST THINGS FIRST

By Bill Ripken

We've all heard the saying "Practice makes perfect," but this is not always true. Dad was always clear in saying that you play the way you practice, so that if you practice the right way, or you practice perfectly, then you're going to play perfectly. A lot of that has to do with being armed with the proper fundamentals and a plan to go out on the field and do things the right way.

If you take 100 ground balls in practice and you field them the wrong way, when ground ball number 101 comes to you in the game, you're going to field that one the wrong way as well. Our approach, using stations, is designed to make more efficient use of everyone's time and to give the players more proper repetitions. The more you do things the wrong way, the more you're apt to do things the wrong way, because you're training yourself that way. So to practice catching a ground ball, first you must be armed with the fundamentals on how to catch a ground ball. Then you must try to carry those out every time you catch a ground ball, so that through repetition you're creating the habit of doing it the right way. We'd rather see a player take twenty-five ground balls the right way than fifty ground balls the wrong way; more is not always better.

The whole spirit of perfect practice and what Dad preached to us as kids is that we want to try to develop good habits. The reason that you practice is to learn how to do it and to train your body to do it the right way. So when you're faced with a similar situation in a game, you'll react to it the right way because you've been practicing it the right way. The purpose of perfect practice is to keep in mind what you're trying to accomplish. Try to be disciplined in each drill so you can develop good habits.

Dad always preached developing good habits. Now that's not to say that you can't have fun in the context of that. A lot of people will make the distinction that if you practice perfectly, that means you're practicing very seriously, which, therefore, takes all the fun out of your practice. That's not true. We're just trying to say there's a right way to do it; you can integrate fun into all your practices, but make sure that the fundamentals of what you're doing—such as the way you field the ground ball—are correct. We're all about having fun. Dad enjoyed being in uniform and enjoyed teaching. Cal and I enjoy being in uniform and enjoy teaching, and we try to integrate fun every way that we can. But never compromise and say, "We're just going to have fun and not do things the right way." Success is always more enjoyable than failure. Practicing the fundamentals of baseball the right way will give us the best chance to succeed and have fun.

KEEP THINGS MOVING

We believe in keeping a practice interactive. We don't want too much standing around. Coaches can figure out how to do things in small work stations or groups. If you're short on coaches, invite other parents to come and help out. Make a hitting station, a throwing station, and a fielding station and try to keep the kids active.

The kids come to practice ready to play. There's a value in organizing them in a group and introducing them to a stretching program where they're in a circle. But don't lose their attention by spending too much time in that stretching mode. Get them in a circle around the mound and let one player lead the stretching exercises. Make the exercises basic so as to introduce the concept that stretching takes place before you play. But young players are resilient—their bodies are like rubber, so they don't need a whole lot of stretching.

Consider working on baserunning first. Instead of having the coach say to the kids, "Run around that goal two miles away and come back," you can conduct a group exercise of running the bases to get loose and get the blood flowing. In our program we tapped into a model that we call Big League

Baserunning. We did that for conditioning in spring training, by running to first base a certain way. The idea is that kids love to run around, so we start our practice off with them running around the bases. It's not a bad idea to let the players catch their breath a little bit and then put them through a little group stretching around the mound so you can talk to them about what you're going to do in practice that day. You can lay out which group goes to which station. The kids are all there and ready to listen to you because you got some of the energy out of them by having them run the bases.

BREAKING IT UP

One thing that can happen at a youth practice with twelve kids on the team is that there'll be eleven standing in the field and one taking batting practice from the coach. Then the coach says, "Next," and there's a revolving door with each player taking five or eight swings. The kids don't get a whole lot out of that. You look around the field and you see most of them digging in the dirt with their cleats or throwing rocks or dirt clods back and forth at each other. That's the exact opposite of what we believe in as far as getting things done and getting things done efficiently.

If you have twelve kids and you get a couple of parents involved to help, you can easily have three subgroups of four. You can bounce the kids around: Four can work on a fielding drill, four can work on a throwing drill, and four can work on a hitting drill. Then shift those around every ten or fifteen minutes. You'll find at the end of the practice that the kids got more out of the smaller groups than they would have if there'd been the typical eleven guys standing in the field with one guy hitting. There are many different drills you can do—outfield, infield, pitching, hitting, baserunning, throwing. The options are endless. The idea is to keep the groups small and keep the kids moving around, which holds their interest. By using smaller groups and rotating them quickly, the players will spend less time standing around and more time actually working on baseball skills.

MANAGING SPACE

We know that a lot of coaches have limited field space. So as a coach you ask yourself, "How do I incorporate various stations with the use of one field to get the most out of our practice?" Let's assume you have one diamond, and you have the backstop. In many cases you can set up a soft-toss or a hitting tee station outside the backstop. And what we like to do is have a fielding/throwing station out in the outfield, where you have four players in a straight line with a fungo hitter. You might start out hitting easy ground balls to them and have them catch the ball and come up throwing to a player or coach standing off to the side, and then rotate so the next player gets his chance. You're occupying their attention in a nice, rhythmic way. Spend no more than ten or fifteen minutes on this drill, and mix in fly balls with ground balls. That's a catching and throwing station because you're letting them practice fielding ground balls and practice fielding fly balls, and in the process they have the space to work on building up momentum to throw the ball a little further because you're spread out in the outfield.

Put another group at the back of the batting cage, where you can have a tee with a number of balls set up, and you can have those players take a number of swings off the tee, or you can set up a soft-toss drill with another coach. They can take ten swings apiece and then you rotate again. That's another ten- to fifteen-minute activity.

THE IMPORTANCE OF HITTING

The station on which you should put a lot of emphasis is live batting practice. We're working off the model of twelve players, so you'll have four kids in that group as well. They each take a turn hitting off the coach who's throwing batting practice. You want to throw from a distance that's comfortable and you want them to be able to hit the ball. The other three players can shag in the outfield and you rotate around. Assuming you have four players in that group, you might want to go sixteen minutes total, four minutes a person. You'll get a lot of swings in four minutes.

So if you divide into three sections and have the players spend sixteen minutes at each station and rotate around, you'll have a practice that will last about forty-five minutes and the players will have a lot of catching, throwing, and swinging the bat. That's how we like to use the field because we place a big emphasis—especially in the early stages—on hitting.

Too many times what we see in practices—and this is probably because coaches don't have enough help or enough baseballs to go around—is coaches who have all their kids go out to their defensive positions; the coach stands at the plate throwing or hitting balls to them and they practice game situations. There's a value to that at a certain point, but that's really occupying everyone's attention with one coach and one ball. If you add up the opportunities that each kid has to catch and throw the ball, it's really minimal. That's one thing that you want to try to avoid. You can have an infield session after your stations, and that can be valuable to explain certain team fundamentals. But if you focus on the stations as the main part of your practice, you'll get forty-five minutes of real quality skillwork.

PLAN AHEAD

A lot of parents volunteer to be coaches. That's great and we encourage it—but remember that you should give some thought to how you're going to run each practice before you go to the field. Don't try to figure it out with all the kids there, getting restless. You'll lose control of your group of kids if you haven't given some thought to how you're going to divide them, what stations are going to take place.

Write some notes down beforehand. It doesn't take long for you to figure out what the game plan will be, even how you're going to group those players into the various stations. The more you do in preparation, the more confidence you'll instill in the kids, the more they'll follow you, and the more you'll have control of your practice.

SHOW THEM HOW

You might want to give a three- to five-minute introduction at each station to show the players exactly what you want done. Visual aid is key in this game. You can tell the kids what you want, but they don't always get it. Sometimes things get lost in translation or in the verbiage that you use. But if you give the players a physical demonstration and they watch it, they can't really lose that in translation.

The verbal cues are still important. You have to give the players reference points on what you want. We try to keep the terms short. For example, what does "Show me the inside of the glove" mean? It means the glove angle has to be the right way. Most kids put their glove flat on the ground and the ball goes up their arm and hits them. If you're a coach at one of our camps and you say, "Show me the inside of the glove," those players know exactly what it means. They heard us say it all summer long. So we get everyone using the same terminology. That's the triggering point.

KEEP YOUR EARS OPEN

We place a big emphasis on having fun and we want to teach the principles and lessons, but at the same time we want to engage the kids and not make practice so strict and rigid that the monotony kills them. And remember to listen to the players. We get a lot of questions from the kids, and we encourage those questions. And we'll have an answer too. Remember: If we don't have an answer, we're not teaching.

Sometimes the players will help you put things in terms they can understand. Often we'll explain something by using other principles in other sports to drive home the point in baseball. At the hitting tee station at one of our camps a player brought up *Happy Gilmore*. That's a movie in which Adam Sandler plays a hockey player who becomes a golfer. There are certain fundamentals of getting behind a slap shot that are similar to getting behind hitting the ball with the bat. Happy Gilmore winds up in that ridiculous fashion that he does and it makes you realize that he uses all of his body in doing that. So when we're trying to describe something like that, we need a way to drive it home to the kids. When you mention *Happy Gilmore,* you find that most kids saw that movie and liked it, so it helps them get the idea. Don't be afraid in this drill with the tee; we want you to transfer your weight to the back side, and you might feel a little ridiculous but think of it like Happy Gilmore.

We find a lot of little jewels like that coming back to us from the kids. If you keep an open mind when you're explaining things and you give the kids a chance to offer some feedback, you'll find that they come up with a lot of really good things. It helps you tap into how they think. Feedback from the players is as important as us giving directions. We like them to throw out the Happy Gilmore–type comments.

GETTING PARENTS INVOLVED

When you're a coach, it behooves you to meet with the parents first, before you meet with the kids. Have a separate parents meeting and lay out your expectations, your philosophies on playing time and winning, and your rules, and then open yourself up. Say, "Look, I need some assistance. I know that a lot of you care about that. I'm not asking for full-time assistance, but I need your assistance. Can we work out a schedule so we can get the most out of each practice?" The more you deal with the parents directly up front, the more you'll gain their support, and they'll gain a level of understanding that'll make your season go a whole lot better.

All you need are two parents to help out at each practice, and that should be pretty easy because the reason the kids are playing and the parents are coming out to the games is that they enjoy the sport and they're supportive. They might not have the time to come out every single week, but we've found that there's almost always more than enough parents who'll help. It's also for supervision and safety. You can explain to the kids the game plan and the purpose of each drill; relieve the parents of that responsibility. All they have to do is make sure they're running the drill the way you'd like them to, and for the kids to get out of the drill or the activity what it was designed to give them. You're looking for volunteers, and if you ask, you'll most likely get the support.

LENGTH OF PRACTICES

Sometimes coaches will ask us with regard to practice time, "How much is too much?" Common sense should play a big factor in that decision. When you have a group of kids, you can tell when you don't have their interest anymore. And if you keep trying to go over things when you don't have their interest, you're damaging the situation because you're not going to get anything in terms of quality out of that as far as trying to work on certain skill sets.

The age group also plays into it. You don't want an eight-year-old on the field for two hours. The older the kids get, the more their attention span grows, the more ability they have to grasp things, and the longer they can do certain things. With younger kids we like to spend a short time at each station, keep them interested, and make it interactive. The more interactive you are with the kids, the more efficient you can be with your time. There's no reason why the younger age groups can't have a quality practice in about forty-five minutes. It keeps them interested, and it makes them want to go back the next week. If you put your eight-year-olds out on the field for two and a half hours and you say to them the next week, "Let's go to practice," they'll remember that two and a half hours and say that wasn't much fun. Keeping the kids interested is the job of the coach, as well as teaching the players the fundamentals. You have to be creative and innovative to help the kids maintain their interest level, and that'll make for a better practice.

If you're looking at the five- to eight-year-old range, you have to make the assumption that you don't have them for a long length of time. Your window of opportunity to teach and their attention span are even smaller. They haven't developed the ability to stay focused on one thing for very long. If you go into a practice not considering that, then you run the risk of not reaching them. The idea of teaching is reaching them. They're more about having fun in the activity than learning the sport. We're going to try to do both. We're going to try to accentuate the fun and try to teach in smaller periods.

So if you're dividing into stations, put yourself into the players' shoes and think, "If I were a five-year-old or an eight-year-old, what would I like to do?" Then bring yourself back to being an adult and ask yourself what you can teach them within the framework of what they like to do. As long as you can find one or two things to teach that age group in the course of that practice—such as fundamental things like throwing and catching—you'll be successful.

Err on the side of too short a practice as opposed to too long a practice. In the five-to-eight age group we recommend no more than a one-hour practice. Baserunning is really fun for them, so you might want to save that till last, or you might want to let them run around the bases early. What you want is that when the practice is over they're all full of energy and happy and they want to stay and throw the ball around. That means that they're doing it on their terms because they like it. That's opposed to saying that practice is going to last two hours and then you see the kids doing other things and not paying attention to you.

In the five-to-eight age range you should assume that there's going to be a small window of opportunity. You might want to rotate your stations a little more frequently: Have ten-minute stations as opposed to twenty-minute stations for the older age groups. You're building a base for the kids to love the game of baseball, so you want them to want to come to your practice.

The nine- and ten-year-olds are going to have a little bit longer attention span and you can start to break things down in a more traditional form of teaching because you might have them a little longer. You can accomplish a lot in an hour or an hour and a half if you do things the right way. Let your team be the judge on the time frame.

At eleven and twelve the players start to have a lot more patience and understanding of the game, so the practices can then become a lot more traditional and you can get a lot more out of them. But again, use common sense as you step up the age ladder.

The same goes with all activities in practice: Common sense and caution should be applied. Keep your eyes open and be prepared to make adjustments. Is the distance too far? Are there any complaints of sore arms? Is the drill just too hard for this group? You're the coach and you have to decide with your own eyes how things are going. Observe, make adjustments as needed, and seek feedback from your players. It's a learning process every day.

Some coaches keep their kids out on the field for two and a half hours because they're trying to accomplish too many things in that one practice. Our belief is that if you want to accomplish five things in a practice and you try to do it all with the whole team at one time, it's not going to work as well. But if you break into groups—maybe even five groups where you can work on each one of those things at one time—you do it more efficiently and you do it more quickly. What you typically see is a team taking batting practice, then infield, then relays and everything else, and they're doing it as one big group. It takes a long time to do it that way. So if you want to accomplish those individual things or some of those items, at least break them down into smaller groups to get the job done.

Dad used to have a saying: "Rome wasn't built in a day." So let's not try to accomplish everything in one practice. If you really do it right and you identify the five things that you'd like the kids to learn at that age group, then you can work toward consistently accomplishing that goal in your practice by game-planning for that year. My recommendation would be to stay consistent with that message and build that every single day so that they start to understand what to expect in practice. Maybe later you can add a little bit on top of that. What we accomplish today will help us have a better practice the next day. Let's identify the five most important things in this particular season that we're going to teach our kids and then stay within that framework and be consistent with that so that by the end of the season they'll have a good grasp of those five things.

PRE-GAME PRACTICE

One of the problems we're seeing these days is that there are more games than practices. If you're playing games all the time and you're trying to get the necessary preparation in for the game, the coach will often get there an hour early because you want your players to get their batting practice in and their throwing in. You're limited in your total stations, but just as in a regular practice, you can get a lot more accomplished if you have support from the parents and you have a couple more coaches.

A lot of youth baseball teams have to deal with the problems of a shortage of playing fields and a lack of warm-up time for their games. For kids to learn how to hit they have to swing the bat. You can't have them take four or five swings at batting practice and say they're ready for a game. And in some leagues they'll just start the game without BP because they're on such a tight schedule with the fields that they don't have time for it.

But with a few simple pieces of equipment you can get a lot accomplished in a limited amount of space and time. One great piece of equipment is a portable hitting screen. It's also worth investing in a batting tee and an automatic soft-toss machine. You can fit all that in your car, and as a coach you can take that equipment to a game or practice and set up two hitting stations: an automatic soft-toss area and a tee area. You can also have a live hitting station if space permits. So if you have twelve kids you can have two or three groups of four working at each station and getting plenty of swings in a very short period of time before the game starts.

There should be a few more practices and fewer games so coaches can work on things in a developmental sense. It seems like the trend has gone to the more games the better. But you can still apply the station concept to your pre-game practice, and the value of that is you get more done in less time so there's less standing around and the kids are more engaged.

As we've said, batting practice is the most important thing you can have, period. The players are only going to get four repetitions in a game situation, and in order to get better as a hitter—and hitting is one of the hardest things to do—you need to have numerous opportunities. So make sure you carve out some sort of batting practice before each game. If you have two screens and you can have two stations, the players can get the time in that way.

In the early ages the situational stuff is less important because the players don't fully understand the game. Once they've played the game for a while they start to understand the situations. A coach can defeat the purpose when he's pounding situation ball into his players when he really should be worried about them catching grounders, catching fly balls, and hitting. You want to simplify the skills that are going to be required for them to move up the ladder.

TEACHING: GAMES VS. PRACTICES

The game's a test, and we don't think coaches should try to teach in the context of the game. Let the kids play the game. Take notes and observe what happens in the game as a test, and after the test is over, the next day at practice, you can pick a time and a way to present that teaching. There's enough pressure, scrutiny, and embarrassment in the game as it is without the coach saying, "We're trying to do this and that."

When he managed in the minor leagues, Dad would sit and watch the games, and if a mistake was made, he wouldn't address that on the bench. He would instead make a note of it, and after the game was over he'd collect all the things he noticed and prepare a one-and-a-half- or two-minute meeting the next day with whichever player was involved. He dealt with those teachings individually, which preserved each player's dignity and didn't single anyone out. It was one on one, and that way he preserved their trust. He would identify the situation but also reinforce what was positive with a clear head. The player would leave with a good bounce in his step. In a way they looked forward to going in there, so it helped the relationship between manager and player individually, and it helped in learning the game.

Some people might say, "Wasn't there value in the lesson for the whole group?" But by doing that you're singling out the individual. There's one benefit that we should point out: When you do it individually, you're arming the kid with more knowledge in the game, and there's a sharing of knowledge that goes on among the kids. When you arm the kid with something that's right and he's in an environment where he witnesses something else, he can actually pass that along and open a discussion. That teaching is going to go around. Some players are going to make more mistakes than others. By continuing to say for the value of the group, "Sam made a mistake yesterday in the game, and let's talk about that so we all know what's going on," well, Sam might make another mistake, and it might start to become a situation in which Sam is identified all the time, which is unfair to him. You can still get the points of the lesson across through your direct teaching.

PLANNING YOUR PRACTICE

John Habyan, who coordinates the pitching instruction for Ripken Baseball, pitched in the major leagues for parts of 11 seasons and has been the head baseball coach at St. John the Baptist High School in West Islip, New York, since 1997. Now that we've described the general guidelines, to help sum up this chapter and provide some practical application we asked Habes to lay out his fundamentals for running a practice and then to map out a sample three-day practice planner based on the schedule he uses for his team (see pages 210–11). These illustrate the points that Habes stresses when he advises other coaches on how to run their practices.

FUNDAMENTALS FOR RUNNING A PRACTICE

1. Organization

- Write your practice plan down before each practice.
- Be well equipped: baseballs, fungo bats, and so on.
- Be on time.
- Purchase a coach's watch.
- Assign a specific amount of time for individual and team drills that you want to work on that day.
- Find a reliable assistant coach.

2. Practice Basics

Plenty of infield and outfield fungos should be a staple of every practice. This does not mean taking infield in the traditional sense, with one ball and four players at their positions in the field. What this does mean is multiple fungo hitters hitting to multiple infielders and outfielders at the same time. You want to get the most out of that time, which means more players doing things at the same time. For example, if you have two fungo hitters on the infield, one can be hitting grounders to the third baseman, who will throw to the second baseman, and one can be hitting fungos to the shortstop, who will throw to the first baseman.

3. Establishing Team Fundamentals

Your core team fundamentals should be established as soon as possible and worked on and polished throughout the season:

- cutoffs and relays
- bunt defense
- first-and-third defense (defensive situations with runners on first and third base)
- baserunning
- pickoffs and rundowns
- communication (using consistent language in situations such as calling for a fly ball)

4. Using Small Groups and Rotations

- Take an efficient batting practice with four stations.
- Work on multiple skills at the same time.

Habes put together the following three-day practice planner based on the schedule that he uses for his team. Habes's practices run three hours apiece, which is a little advanced for younger players; for the purposes of this model he condensed the schedule to two hours. But this is just a working model. A coach has to feed off his players and adjust the schedule based on which areas need work. The key is being organized and including a variety of fundamentals while keeping things moving.

Three-Day Sample Practice Schedule

Day 1

3:00–3:20	Stretch, run, and throw
3:20–3:40	Infield and outfield fungos
3:40–4:00	Cutoffs and relays
4:00–4:20	Baserunning
4:20–5:00	Batting practice (four ten-minute stations: live hitting, tee, and two shag stations); pitchers throw on the side

Day 2

3:00–3:20	Stretch, run, and throw
3:20–3:40	Infield and outfield fungos
3:40–4:00	Cutoffs and relays (incorporating baserunning)
4:00–4:20	Live stealing drill
4:20–5:00	Batting practice (four ten-minute stations: bunting, soft toss, tee, and two shag stations); pitchers throw on the side

Day 3

3:00–3:20	Stretch, run, and throw
3:20–3:40	Infield and outfield fungos
3:40–4:00	Pickoffs and rundowns
4:00–4:20	First-and-third defense
4:20–5:00	Intersquad game

LESSONS LEARNED

Winning and Losing

By Cal Ripken, Jr.

'm on the corporate speaking circuit now, and when I give a speech I always identify the principles to which I aspired in baseball and try to draw a parallel to the business world. I'm getting better at making that connection between sports and business. One of the topics that I discuss is the value of winning and losing.

Obviously everyone wants to be a winner, but for a lot of people the focus on winning is so great that it clouds their perspective. Learning takes place regardless of the outcome. Some would say that you learn more from your failures and your losses than you do from winning. That may be true, but the most important thing to remember with regard to youth sports is that winning should come second to the development of the kids.

There's a time and a place to worry about winning and employing strategy, and that's when everyone has learned enough of the skills to compete. As I've gone through the experience of watching my own kids develop in sports, I've witnessed many examples of coaches and parents who are blinded by winning—to the point where winning takes precedence over personal development, teaching, sportsmanship, and having fun.

I offer my opinion as a warning of sorts. I hope everyone who reads this will reexamine and rethink the purpose and the value of youth sports. I recently read a book called *Why Johnny Hates Sports,* by Fred Engh, that hits this issue right between the eyes. It's well written in a style that's easy to read and understand. I wholeheartedly recommend it to everyone involved in youth sports, and even if you're not involved in youth sports I think it has tremendous value.

Winning and losing are always going to be topics to deal with when teaching sports. Once we've adopted the right philosophy, we have to manage the process, and that means dealing with certain behaviors and situations. How about the kid who's so competitive and who wants to win so badly that when things go wrong he throws a fit? How do you deal with this? Well, I have a little insight on this one. I was that kid who threw fits. I have a son, Ryan, who acts just like I did when I was his age. It's funny how things can come back to haunt you as a parent.

We've all witnessed how kids react to winning and losing. Depending on their makeup, some kids accept things and move on and others have a tougher time understanding their feelings. I use the words *understanding their feelings* because to me that's precisely the issue. Kids learn how to catch, throw, shoot, or pass, and as coaches we understand that their successes and mistakes are all part of development. We don't seem to look at behavior issues the same way, but I think we should. When a kid throws a fit on the sports field, it's rarely about his behavior. It's more about a reaction to something within the sport that he doesn't have the capacity or experience to deal with. It could be frustration caused by his own lack of success; it could be frustration caused by his team's lack of success. There's a good chance that it's frustration of some sort. That's the mental side of sports. We need to teach the kids how to be good winners and how to cope with their failures and their losses.

My parents and my brothers and sister had to deal with me growing up. I was the worst winner (I loved to brag) and the all-time worst loser (talk about fits and tantrums). I was a pretty good athlete, so I won a lot (bad for everyone around me), and I didn't have to face losing that often. But when I did lose at something, boy, did I get it from all sides. And I didn't react too well. Over time and with a lot of guidance and support from my parents I was able to cope with winning and losing much better. I still don't like losing, but I've learned how to deal with it.

If you were to ask me, "How did my parents help me?," I couldn't exactly lay it out for you. I know they were patient. I know they explained things well. I know they gave me tools to deal with my feelings. But I can't duplicate their blueprint exactly. I can, however, tell you the lessons I learned when my son began to act like I did when I was a kid.

When Ryan started to play sports, it was obvious that he had an incredible passion for competition. But when things didn't go well, he would get mad, cry, pout, and want to run away. My inclination was to be tough with him. I made the mistake of getting a little angry, and I said things like "Just suck it up," or "That's not the way we act." I guess I was reacting to my own feelings of embarrassment for his behavior. But once I thought about it, I realized that it wasn't about me. It was about Ryan and his ability—or, better yet, his lack of ability— to deal with his powerful feelings.

Once I realized what was going on I developed a strategy to help him. I waited for a time to talk to him when things were quiet, when he was calm and away from the ball field. I started off by asking him why he thought he behaved like he did. He said, "I don't know. I just get so worked up that I can't control myself." I told him that I understood because I was the same way when I was his age. He liked hearing that. I told him that his feelings were a special gift that means that he cares more than others. That gift is a strong force that's going to be helpful to you, I said, but you have to learn how to manage it. You need to use it for good things. You need to channel it back into your sport and let it help you play better. For instance, when you get mad, instead of throwing a fit, use that anger to help you swing or play defense. You can feel how strong it is when it starts to come out. Try to make that power work for you when you're playing.

Now this sounds good, but it doesn't completely fix the problem. This is just the first step in a long process. I've laid the groundwork for Ryan to start to figure out how he can use

his feelings for an advantage. I'm going to be there to help remind him when he gets overwhelmed, but the important
thing is that as he learns the physical part of the game he'll be
growing mentally and emotionally as well.

I believe that these strong, competitive feelings are a positive. I've talked to a lot of parents who see them as a huge negative. They would like nothing better than for their child to
try to suppress those feelings. They see it as a behavior flaw.
But passion is a great thing in athletics. I'll take the player
who cares and has that fire inside every time over the player
you have to motivate and try to get interested. It all starts at
the grass roots.

Sometimes it's a simple matter of making things fun. Here's
an example: One day Ryan's soccer team was handed a crush-
ing defeat. Both teams played really well and it was a close
game. It's the kind of game that the parents can't even watch
because they agonize right along with their kids. At one point
I shouted out a little encouragement to Ryan and his teammates after the other team went ahead. I said, "Hey, that's all
right. You guys are playing great. Keep it up." I got a really bad
look from my boy. Later I found out from him that I had
cheered at the wrong time. He took it as if I were rooting for
the other team. (I told you I have my hands full, didn't I?)

The game ended with Ryan's team losing by that one goal.
After the game Ryan wouldn't talk to me, and it was obvious
to all in attendance that he wasn't happy. In fairness to Ryan
there were many members of his team who were unhappy and
pouting. At that point I came up with an idea. I walked to the
middle of the field with a soccer ball and punted it straight up
in the air as high as I could. When the ball came down, I had
one kid come over. I did it again and then five kids were
around me. By the third time most all the kids on Ryan's team
had come over. Ryan joined in on the fun and a pickup game
broke out between the parents and their kids. We played for
about a half an hour. I had a blast, and the other parents did
as well. You know by now that the kids had a great time, too.

What I discovered that day was that there were no words in the English language that could have produced those results. It was amazing how quickly Ryan and the rest of the kids moved on to another activity and forgot about the tough loss. It made for a wonderful ride home, and all we invested was thirty minutes of having fun with our kids. The lesson here is that communication with our kids can take many forms. We related to the kids this time by thinking and acting like them.

Here's another example. I've observed a cool thing watching my little man's team during the past two summers: They just love to run around the bases. When the team wins, they celebrate by running around the bases. Before and after practice they run around the bases. I thought I would take advantage of this joy and apply it in two more places. At the start of every practice we warm up with what we call Big League Baserunning. I introduced the exact spring training ritual we used with the Orioles. It accomplishes a few things: First, it serves as a warm-up to get the body ready for practice. Second, it's a teaching opportunity. It also burns off some of the excess energy that boys generally have, and it puts them in a little better learning mode. Finally, it can simply be a lot of fun.

The second application for running the bases was put in place after a loss. After witnessing the joy the kids displayed running the bases after a win, I thought it would serve as a good way to move on after a loss. Kids can recover quickly if you simply give them something fun to do. I talked to the coach and he agreed to give it a try. Most of the time after a loss we would try to have a meeting. I believe this happens because this is a parent's or a coach's attempt to console and support. Our kids feel bad, so we'd better get them together and talk to them. I believe a meeting after a loss tends to add fuel to the fire of their sad feelings. All it really does is remind them why they're sad. Instead, change the activity. Change the subject. Run the bases and have fun. I'm proud to announce that it worked. We all had better car rides home after the games. The lessons from the game can be discussed at a later time when the kids have cooled down.

TOURNAMENTS

In a 2003 interview with *Sports Illustrated* I talked about the ten-year-old athlete. Since my son Ryan is ten years old, the writer thought it would be a good idea to get my perspective on the subject. I basically said that at Ryan's age winning should not be the focus, that teaching and learning how to play the game should be the primary concern. It was a wonderfully positive article and was well received by most parents and coaches. It did, however, prompt a skeptical response that was printed in the letters section of the magazine a few weeks later. The letter essentially said that on one hand Cal is saying that winning doesn't matter but on the other hand he has a whole league named after him that crowns a champion of a World Series for nine- and ten-year-olds. The letter went on to say that it sounds as if Cal is speaking out of both sides of his mouth.

When my friends first showed me this response in *SI*, I shrugged it off. As Dad would always say, that's just his opinion; it doesn't make it fact. It was obvious that the reader didn't know about our goals for our league and our World Series. But then it hit me: This was less about me and more about the reader's definition—and probably his own experiences—of youth baseball and tournaments.

It was obvious that this reader saw tournaments as a negative thing. That was my first reaction as well. One could say that they're all about winning. But do they have to be all about winning? A game is ultimately about winning, so does that make it a negative as well? What if we change our way of looking at games and tournaments? What if we define tournaments and games as simply the structures in which baseball is played? After all, it's not the tournaments or the games themselves that tell us how we should play them. It's the people who create them. These people are the coaches, the parents, the league administrators, the event organizers, and even the players themselves. It's all of us. We provide the direction. We can decide how we want the games and the tournaments to be played. We can emphasize teaching, sportsmanship, and teamwork if we want to.

I recently learned a lesson about providing the right direction as it applied to my home basketball games. Basketball has always been my way of staying in shape in the off-season, and it continues to be a sport I enjoy on a regular basis. I guess it would be safe to say that since I retired from baseball I've poured my competitive juices into basketball. My friends and I play at my gym about three times a week. Over the years the talent level has continued to rise and the games have become very competitive. I liked that very much, but at one point I started to notice that our games had a lot more hard fouls (intentional as well) and a lot more arguing. It had become a matter of winning at all costs. I let the behavior go for a while, thinking that this was just the by-product of having better players. But the games became a lot less fun. One day I got mad and basically turned off the lights and said, "The games are over. Go home."

I blamed myself, though, for not providing the direction to the players. This was my gym (I was, in effect, the tournament director) and I hadn't communicated my expectations. The game governed itself and it became something undesirable. I scheduled a game about a week later, and this time I communicated what I expected. This isn't club-style basketball, I said, where survival is all about winning and staying on the court. This is about playing hard, playing fair, and ultimately about having fun. I was the tournament director laying down the law for a successful tournament. The games are now a success.

Tournaments can be a lot like my pickup basketball games. If you don't identify the purpose and direction of a tournament, you won't get the desired results. When I was first exposed to the tournament structure with Ryan I didn't like it at all. He was seven or eight and the tournaments provided additional games for his team. It seemed as if there was a tournament every other weekend. My wife, Kelly, and I picked up on a change in the behavior and attitude of the team. They became overly excited. The conversations between innings turned to "If we win today, we play a doubleheader tomorrow," or "If we lose today, we're in the losers' bracket." They would try harder. The frustration level would build and ultimately the pressure would increase. This is a lot for young kids to deal with. There was more crying, more yelling, and much more disappointment. This is not the kind of environment in which you want your child learning to play baseball.

It was easy to blame the tournament. It was easy to focus on that structure of winners' and losers' brackets to explain the behavior. But here's where I learned a lesson: Not all the teams were being affected the same way. There were a couple of teams on which all the kids were having fun. No, it wasn't the teams that were winning all the games. I searched out the coaches of those teams to find out their secret. It was all about the direction they set for their teams, their season, and the tournaments. These teams competed within the structure of the games, but it was obvious that the goal wasn't winning at all costs—it was teaching the kids how to compete and play and give their best effort, and giving the kids a positive experience. These coaches did a great job of communicating their goals, philosophies, and expectations to the kids and their parents. They built their own model within the structure of the game, the league, and the season. The kids understood and followed the direction and the behavior of their coaches. They learned, they played, and they had fun regardless of the outcome of the games. It opened my eyes. They proved that the power is truly in the hands of the coaches, parents, and players, and not in the format of the games or tournaments. With the right philosophy and the right direction, youth baseball tournaments can be a great and beneficial experience.

It's in this spirit that we created the philosophy for our World Series. When Babe Ruth renamed its younger division Cal Ripken Baseball worldwide, it gave us a wonderful opportunity to affect the grass roots of baseball directly. Big league players can claim to have a positive effect on kids just by showing a good example, but having a whole league affords us the chance to do bigger things. I'm sure I could just be a figurehead to Babe Ruth and sit back and accept the honor of having a league named after me, but where's the fun in that? We want to be a part of growing the game, and that starts at the youth level, so we're going to be as hands-on as Babe Ruth will allow.

Since the name was changed to Cal Ripken Baseball, we've had four World Series. In 2003 we brought the World Series to what we hope will be its permanent spot, our hometown of Aberdeen, Maryland. At each of the World Series we addressed the coaches, players, and families at a banquet on the evening before the start of the games. It's important to us that all the participants understand what we're trying to accomplish during this event.

That speech is about celebrating and enjoying the whole experience. This is a life experience; it's not all about the crowning of a world champion. One team will win the tournament, that's a fact, but how will everyone look back on this time twenty years from now? Will the participants remember it as a good experience that helped shape them as people? An experience that helped broaden their horizons? An experience that they can share with their kids and hope they have similar experiences in their lives? We encourage the kids to open up to the players on the other teams and get to know them. We try to schedule additional activities and baseball skills competitions that put the teams together. The teams come from all over the world. We want everyone to take advantage of this unique opportunity to learn about people and the places where they live. We try to identify other values within the Series besides winning the final game.

Last year we discovered a real value that we could add for the teams that didn't advance to the next round. Our facility was nearing completion and some of the other field areas were usable. We wanted to test our brand-new training infield, so we invited all the kids whose teams had been eliminated from the tournament to an impromptu private clinic. The results were fantastic. We at Ripken Baseball got to see our training infield in full use and the kids had a fantastic time. The greatest benefit of this clinic happened by accident. The kids who were out of the tournament were a bit bummed out. We were able to turn those frowns into smiles in a heartbeat. The parents and coaches gathered around and energized us all. The teams that were still in the tournament felt a little deprived and left out, but we were able to enhance the overall experience by adding additional baseball for those other teams.

Within the structure of our league and World Series we continue to look for ways to improve the experience for the kids. Games and tournaments don't have to conflict with our principles and goals for teaching and having fun. We have the ability to make the games and tournaments work for us in the way we want them.

TEAM MEETINGS

I remember how I felt about meetings at the big league level. I wasn't crazy about them in general, but I especially disliked the yell-and-scream variety after a loss. Meetings in preparation for the game can be beneficial. Meetings just for the sake of meetings can be destructive. Meetings become more important at the higher levels, but at the lower levels we have to exercise good judgment on when to meet.

When dealing with kids you must take into consideration their attention span and their emotional maturity. Kids are generally about action and less about talk. Meetings are tools for the adults. They're a way to exchange necessary information, to communicate. Adults can communicate through words and through their actions. Kids tend to communicate more through their actions. The expression "Actions speak louder than words" is true for all ages, but it especially applies to young kids.

Most of the meetings that I've witnessed in youth sports occur to discuss players' mistakes or to deal with a loss. Frustration seems to be the motivating force. Watching kids come out of these meetings with their heads down really bothers me. They look as though they've been scolded for doing something bad. You hear things like "We made way too many mental mistakes today. That's inexcusable," or "I don't know where your minds were today, but it sure wasn't on baseball or this game," or "We just lost our focus. That team didn't beat us, we beat ourselves," or "I want you to go home and think about this game and how bad we played, and maybe we'll wake up next time."

Ryan's coach this year had a really good way of summing up a game. He gathered his team briefly and identified some positive accomplishments, and he awarded a game baseball after each game. We see this in football quite a lot at all levels, but I hadn't seen it in baseball. He had a little ceremony—he presented a baseball inscribed with the date and the name of the kid and he announced it to the team. The players would wait in anticipation and clap for the winner. The coach had decided that every kid would win a game ball that season. He looked for positive contributions every game and would try to award the ball to a less talented kid early in the season because he wanted to make sure the child felt it was deserved. It could be a great and unexpected catch, or just being tough by staying in the game after getting hit with a pitch, or drawing a key walk; these are the things that usually don't win awards. This coach made the kids feel good about their contributions. The smiles on their faces were priceless.

Informational meetings are necessary to give the parents and players the latest information on practice times and the next scheduled game. I would suggest getting these meetings out of the way early, before the game starts, to avoid the moods that might follow after a loss, when the kids will not be very attentive and the parents want to leave the field as soon as possible. E-mail is a great way to communicate with the parents for scheduling practices and game times. Coaches might consider a dry-erase board that can be displayed at the field and that has the next game or schedule information already written down. That way parents and kids can refer to it on their own time and a post-game meeting is not necessary.

TEACHING IN GAMES

One lesson that we at Ripken Baseball learned early on was there are better times than others in which to teach. We were so gung ho on passing along the craft of the game to the kids that we thought every opportunity was a teaching opportunity. We were wrong.

When we were in Hawaii a few years ago conducting our camps, things were moving along well. Our model consists of instructional stations in the mornings and games in the afternoons. I moved around the camp and rotated through all the stations. At game time our plan was to spread our instructors around and have them sit on the bench with the players. We know that there are many learning opportunities during the games, and we didn't want to miss out on any. The idea was for the instructors to identify the learning moments in the game and share them with the players on the bench while the game was in progress. But we quickly found out that the players' minds were totally on the game. It was hard for them to switch out of game mode to learning mode, then back to the game.

When we met at the end of the day to assess and compare notes, we decided to take another approach. We still valued the lessons that pop up during the games, but this time we decided to make notes and present them at a later time. This approach worked well because we were able to identify those learning moments, we had time to think and develop the best way to address those moments, and we picked the best times when the kids were receptive to the teaching.

We thought that because the games were practice games of sorts, they would be a good environment to explain and teach. They weren't, though, because the game responsibilities took priority over the learning responsibilities. That's not to say that learning doesn't take place in games. (I'll address that type of learning in a minute.) It just means that fundamental skills and strategies are better to address at a much later time so they can be understood. It was an important discovery for us, and by separating the game from the instruction we were able to reach the kids much better.

So if that's the case with our camp games, what do you think happens in real games? Games are for the kids to experience the good and bad. We can prepare them for the games, and then it's in their hands. My recommendation would be to resist the temptation to teach during the games. Bring a little note-book to the field and make notes of things you see. Take those notes home and develop a plan or lesson on how you can help the kids. Most of the time these notes will lead to individual lessons, but if enough of the same mistakes are being made you can work up a team lesson that will benefit everyone.

Some coaches get so wrapped up in every pitch of a baseball game that they're barking out commands the whole game. They're trying to be the eyes for everyone on the field. Just think about all those commands from the kids' perspective. It's embarrassing to have your name called out loudly and then be told what to do. They feel they're being singled out. They don't know that the coach is just trying to help them.

Most of the time when a coach yells out it's a criticism of sorts. He's identifying something that went wrong in order to fix it. But at the spur of the moment, when a kid is being corrected verbally, I don't think he can be open to the lesson. Kids, especially young kids, are not mature enough to accept the criticism even though it's in the spirit of being positive. (Adults, for that matter, have a tough time with it.) We as coaches need to be as even-keel as we can. Now let's get back to the learning that takes place when you let the kids experience the game. We as parents and coaches have a tendency to want to protect the kids during the games. When your child makes a mistake or commits an error, you want to come to the rescue. You want to make it all right. Despite all the reasons that you might want to interject yourself into the game, don't. Great value and learning take place in the game. Let the experience of the game flow. Let the players experience it uninterrupted.

A good friend of mine made the analogy of a student learning to play a stringed instrument. In practice the teacher works hard on finger placement and bow direction, because they're critical to forming the notes, but when it's time for the recital the teacher just lets go and allows the student to experience the moment. That moment in baseball is the game. Let all those practices come to life on their own. Let the child interpret the flow of the game. Let him feel what it's like to perform under the pressure of an audience. Let him tap into the courage that's required just to try. There's a special type of learning that comes from the actual experience. As parents and coaches, if we interject ourselves into the games we're interfering with that learning. Step back and let the kids play. I refer to this as returning the games to the kids. I know I've mentioned this a couple of times already, but it's well worth mentioning again: We as adults, coaches, and parents need to act as if everything that happens on the field was expected, as if we've seen it a hundred times and nothing surprises us. This sort of reaction enables the kids to play the game more freely and allows them to experience all the great lessons in sports.

THE DANGER OF CHEERING TOO MUCH

I want to share a story with you that might catch you by surprise. When I go to my kids' games I'm particularly sensitive to the environment in which the game is played. I watch the coaches and the parents' behavior before, during, and after the games. I look for the parent who yells negative things from the stands or the coach who overreacts and criticizes his players. After all, that's what most of us feel is wrong with youth sports. This type of behavior intimidates and harms the kids. This is very obvious. "Silent Sundays"—days on which parents and coaches aren't allowed to cheer—were one league's way of dealing with this type of negativity. But I've identified another type of behavior that has the same effect on kids. It's the over-the-top cheering type of parent or coach.

A couple of years ago Ryan had a game against another team of eight-year-olds. I was still playing and I had a chance to see a game early in the morning on a Saturday. I watched the game a little removed from the stands, down the right field line. Ryan's team got off to a rough start and the other team scored six runs in the first couple of innings. The other team's parents and coaches were going crazy, yelling out in support of their players. It was all positive stuff but way too much. I remember the coach walking halfway out on the field and pointing at one of his players who had just gotten a big hit and screaming, "You're the man! Way to swing that bat! That was a big hit! Yeah, yeah, yeah!"

I started to notice the effect that this type of cheering had on Ryan's team, particularly the pitcher, who burst into tears. He had to come out of the game. The celebrations continued on the other side. But the game suddenly took a turn, and Ryan's team made a miraculous comeback and won. During the last inning the other team could do nothing right. All that loud celebration turned to dead silence. The parents and the coaches weren't shouting negative things; they were simply saying nothing at all. The other team came off the field hanging their heads. That silence had the same effect as yelling negative things. They weren't getting that over-the-top positive reinforcement now. It was silent and that silence spoke volumes. They walked off as if they had done something wrong, and I felt bad for them.

The lesson I learned that day was that coaches and parents need to support at a consistent level. They control the emotions of the players. They can drive the kids' emotions way up and they can help them crash. We have to respond to all situations as if we knew they would happen. After all, that should be the value of our life experience.

INDEX

Page numbers in *italics* refer to illustrations.

ABOUT THE AUTHORS

CAL and **BILL RIPKEN** are co-owners of Ripken Baseball, and their mission is to grow the game of baseball worldwide. They recently opened the Ripken Youth Baseball Academy in their hometown of Aberdeen, Maryland. Cal Ripken, Jr., holds one of baseball's most respected records: He played in a record-setting 2,632 consecutive games, surpassing Lou Gehrig's streak of 2,130 straight games, which was thought to be unbeatable. The American League Rookie of the Year in 1982, the AL's Most Valuable Player in 1983 and 1991, and an All-Star nineteen times (the most in AL history), he is one of only seven players in Major League history with 400 homers and 3,000 hits. Bill Ripken is a twelve-year Major League veteran who played for the Baltimore Orioles, Cleveland Indians, Texas Rangers, and Detroit Tigers.

LARRY BURKE is the baseball editor of *Sports Illustrated* and the author of three books on the sport.

**If you liked this book and want more from Ripken Baseball,
sign up for our free *Coach's Clipboard* e-newsletter!**

The e-newsletter features coaching tips from Cal and Bill Ripken,
injury prevention ideas, information on new equipment innovations,
and a chance to share your ideas with the Ripkens and other coaches.

**Log on to www.ripkenbaseball.com
For additional information on Ripken Baseball youth camps
or coaches' clinics, call 1-800-486-0850.**

**The Cal Ripken, Sr. Foundation is helping disadvantaged kids
discover the joys of baseball and softball and assisting coaches
in their efforts to help enhance children's lives.**

**To learn more about the foundation, log on to:
www.ripkenfoundation.org
or call 1-877-RIPKEN-1**